FOOD INSPIRES DESIGN

FOOD
INSPIRES
DESIGN

GRANDMA'S
DESIGN

stichting
kunstboek

GRANDMA'S DESIGN FOOD INSPIRES DESIGN

Grandmothers and designers: they seem to belong to different worlds and yet they are brought together here, in this book. What follows is a journey through time and across borders: grandmothers invite you to visit different countries in Europe by sharing their culinary habits, recipes and histories. At the same time, a designer reinterprets each recipe, creating an incentive to dive into the exciting world of food design.

This book is the result of a project coordinated by npo Vol-au-Vent, that started from a simple idea: bringing together recipes from different countries and revitalising them by turning them into something new. Why baking recipes? Because they possess a strong emotional value: baking is related to the 'home', to happy moments, celebrations and special occasions. In order to grasp that emotional aspect, we appealed to the grandmothers: each of them shares a recipe with a story, one that is rooted in tradition, either concerning the personal sphere, or the history of the country or the region where they live. For the search for grandmothers, Vol-au-Vent appealed to different organizations in the participating countries: Belgium, Italy, Finland, Turkey and The Netherlands. Among them were universities with a background in culinary history (Yeditepe University, Hogeschool van Amsterdam), culinary authors, (Marc De Clercq, Pieter De Clercq) and experienced researchers (Accademia Italiana della Cucina Mediterranea, National Consumer Research Centre Finland).

Eighty-four grandmothers were interviewed and filmed while preparing their authentic recipes, which are all presented on the website 'www.grandmasdesign.com'. With the launch of the website and the organisation of a workshop on food design, professional designers were invited to take part in the food design competition organised by our partner European Design Centre (EDC). Designers from all over the world, from Belgium to Brazil and from Slovakia to Singapore, accepted the challenge to revive a European eating tradition. Even though the combination of food and design might seem unusual at first sight, the complete eating experience has always been of particular interest to the design sector (kitchens, utensils, home appliances...).

Design Flanders not only used its network and skills to search for designers in the region, but also to produce this really attractive publication. The design concepts and recipes selected in this book give you a taste of the wealth of food traditions as well as the creativity and the scope of the area of food design.

Both Food Inspires Design and the Grandma's Design project were rendered possible with the support of the European Culture Programme and thanks to the efforts of our partners: The European Design Centre, who organised a workshop on Food Design and organised the competition; the Associazione culturale Culter, which was responsible for the website; and the Accademia Italiana della Cucina Mediterranea, which conducted the research for the Italian grandmothers.

Food Inspires Design is the last official stop in the Grandma's Design project, although it is not the final destination: An online community is actively engaged in the project through social media (find us on Facebook!), there will be exhibitions (starting in the House of Alijn in Ghent, Belgium) and the recipes will continue to be prepared, hopefully in your kitchen too. Finally we would like to thank all the grandmothers and all the designers for taking part in this project.

We wish you great reading pleasure.

Hilde Brepoels **VZW VOL-AU-VENT**
Johan Valcke **DESIGN VLAANDEREN**

Content

⊌ Winner   ★ Honourable Mention

FRANCESCA ZAMPOLLO   08
Introducing Food Design

ROSA'S APPLE PIE WITH APRICOTS   14
Amélia Desnoyers → Homemade/Handmade ⊌

CANAN'S SAMSA   22
Claire Chuniaud, Tiphaine Rolland and Claire Cheverry → Tatly

SERAFINA'S CASTAGNOLE   30
Roel Vandebeek → Grandma Serafina's Castagnoles

ADRIANA'S CINDERELLA CAKE   38
Sofia Badoui, Anne-Axelle Bouilly and Marie Visonneau → Ipad User Recipe ⊌

LIISA'S KARELIAN PIES   46
Federico Poggioli and Joanne Lin → Kruisp

LUCIA'S BOJO   54
Karla Rosales → Bojo Cake-Tail

ANNIE'S SNOWSTAR   62
Ana Maria Jimenez Amaro → Serving Sweet Magic ⊌

GOEDELE'S FLEMISH WAFFLES   70
Kyung Lim → Deconstructed Benedict ★
Caroline Dobbs → Sugar Sprinkler

MAHMURE'S RAISIN BREAD   82
Eva Závodná → Community Bakery ⊌

EMRIYE'S TWISTED BAKLAVA WITH HAZELNUTS   90
Manolya Isik → How to make Baklava

ANNIE & MARTHA'S QUICK-READY CAKE   98
Hannah Vranko → Quick-Ready Cake Roof ★

FATMA'S KATMER   106
Cyril Leroux, Eléonore Samier and Romain Vince → Mama

ORETTA'S RICOTTA & WILD CHERRY TART   114
Antonella Mignacci → Ricotta & Wild Cherry Tart

GABY'S JAN IN A BAG   122
Léa Bougeault and Jessica Pigeron → Jan in a Bag

MILJA'S BILBERRY RYE PIE   130
Raija Niemi → Bilberry Rye Pie Cakes

GIOVANNINA'S GALUCIU   138
Alice Conquand, Caroline Fourier and Alexandre Leduc → Like Grandma ★

ANNIE'S PEPERNOTEN   146
Satu Lustig → Peperpack-Packaging Concept for Pepernoten

BEPPA'S HAPPINESS CAKE   154
Florin Alexa-Morcov → Clockwork Cake

LIA'S SORRENTINA LEMON TART   162
Alice Dansey-Wright → Sorrentina Lemon Furoshiki

FRANCA'S PASTIERA   168
Antonella Mignacci → Pastiera

SILVANA'S CALABRESE PIZZA   176
Juliana Mendonça , Renata Dias and Larissa Grace → Fray

MAGDA'S SPECULAAS FROM HASSELT   182
Julie Ganaye and Marine Hérisson → Magda

THE JURY   190

Introducing Food Design

Francesca Zampollo

What is Food Design? One of the best ways to differentiate what is Food Design from what is not, is to remember that Food Design is a *Design* discipline. If there is a Design element, a deliberate and reasoned process that produces solutions that satisfy needs and give meanings to our lives, then we are indeed talking about Food Design. In the past 20 years, the term Food Design has been used more and more often, and now refers to anything from sandwiches, to designer cutleries or dishes from the culinary arts.

But what does Food Design mean? Sonja Stummerer and Martin Hablesreiter give their definition in the book *Food Design XL*: *For us the notion of 'food design' refers to the development and sharing of food. In our understanding this includes all the processes and decisions related to successfully designing food in a reproducible and recurring way (p.13).* This definition relates to food products for mass production. With its reference to designing food in a reproducible and recurring way, however, this definition could be reductive. Food Design is more than this.

Stefano Maffei and Barbara Parini, on the other hand, in their book *FoodMood* present four sessions in which they divide the product and services they describe in the book: *foodpeople, foodexperience, foodproducts,* and *foodspecials*. The four sessions can describe an additional effort to categorize the vast world of Food Design. What is particularly interesting is the session *foodpeople*, which presents chefs and their creations. The approach taken in this book is an example of the view that considers chefs as food designers. In describing the reasons why they focus on haute cuisine chefs, the authors explain that *[...] their function is to design on the bases of knowledge, skills, genealogies, memories and personal experiences of processes of transformation that range from the specific to the systematic (p.12).*

This approach to Food Design brings out an additional understanding of the definition of Food Design: Sonja Stummerer and Martin Hablesreiter described Food Design as food designed in a reproducible and recurring way, and Stefano Maffei and Barbara Parini include chef's creations as examples of Food Design. These two approaches demonstrate that Food Design is difficult to define, and most importantly it encompasses categories of products, dishes and services very different from one another. A quick search of the words 'food design' on any search engine produces a multitude of web pages on very different products and services: shapes of pasta, industrial ice cream, chocolate, bottles, cutlery, chairs and tables, the entire eating space like restaurants and cafés, and dishes created by chefs including those operating within the so called *molecular gastronomy*. All these products are very different from one another, in the material itself, in the function they solve, and in the background discipline that creates the knowledge used to design them.

As part of my involvement in the Food Design world, as founder of the International Food Design Society, I have contributed to the understanding of Food Design creating a categorization of its sub-disciplines. These create an overview of the background knowledge from which Food Design can be approached, and shows how different background disciplines create different products and services. This categorization does not aim at setting once and for all the different facets of Food Design, but is instead a first approach towards the understanding of the complexity of this discipline. The aim is to show how Food Designers may approach this discipline depending on their own background knowledge. Nonetheless, this is open to debate, and more importantly, this is open to further interpretation.

The six possible sub-disciplines of Food Design are Design With Food, Design For Food, Food Space Design or Interior Design For Food, Food Product Design, Design About Food, and finally, Eating Design.

Design With Food is the design that melts, swells, blows, foams and reassembles food as a raw material, transforming it to create something that did not exist before in terms of flavour, consistency, temperature, color and texture. Design With Food is about the manipulation of food itself, and considers only food itself as the material used in the design. The food designer in this case is usually the chef or the food scientist. An example of Design With Food is *Èspesso* by Ferran Adrià and Lavazza. *Èspesso* is a coffee lighter than a mousse but firmer than foam (see Figure 1). Ferran Adrià played with the consistency of normal coffee to create a new way of drinking espresso. Another example by Ferran Adrià is *Fruit Caviar*, a creation that looks exactly like caviar, but tastes like fruit, thanks to a process called *sferificacion* invented by Adrià himself. Design With Food is about reinventing the idea of food itself and stimulating the eating experience by twisting sensory expectations.

Design For Food is the design of all the products designed to cut, chop, mix, contain, store, cook and preserve food.
The packaging, for example, is not only the container, but also the means to communicate the product, make it recognizable, and protect it. One of the most successful examples of a product being identified by its container is probably Coca Cola (Figure 2). The silhouette of the glass bottle has become an icon, and a symbol of identification that has made Coca Cola recognizable since 1886. Another product designed *for* food is for example Juicy Salif by Philippe Stark for Alessi, the orange squeezer that has become an icon of product design, with its unique design and spidery legs.

③

⑤

④

Food Space Design or **Interior Design For Food** is about the design of food spaces considering all the characteristics of the eating environment, such as interiors, materials and colors, lighting, temperature and music. Interior Design For Food is the design of the interiors of food spaces such as for examples kitchens, bakeries, patisseries, bars and restaurants. In this category, as in Design For Food, food is not the material to design with, but many of the considerations and knowledge necessary to design an eating space, are about food: from food preparation for an understanding of the better material to design a work top with, to the dynamics of the eating experience, in order to be able to design the correct light, temperature and colors for a specific eating environment. A couple of interesting examples of Food Space Design are the *Restaurant in the Sky* and the *Duvet Restaurant*. The former is a restaurant/dining space for 22 guests who dine suspended 100 feet above the ground. The latter is a New York City restaurant where customers dine laying on beds instead of sitting at a table. Two extreme examples of how the eating environment can create an entirely unique eating experience.

Food Product Design is closer to the idea of the designer as inherently part of an industrial process. Food Product Design is about designing edible mass-produced products. An example of Food Product Design is *Pringles* (see Figure 3), a chemical-physical-morphological design where the chip has an ergonomic shape that perfectly lies on the tongue, releasing its flavor and enhancing the tasting experience. These chips are designed not only to create a strong flavor experience, but also to make it last as long as possible. Another very interesting example is the *Cookie Cup* from Lavazza (see Figure 4), designed by Luis Sardi for the 1st Food Design® competition in 2002.

Cookie Cup is a cup for espresso coffee made of pastry with an internal layer of icing sugar, which works as an insulator, making the cup waterproof but also sweetening the coffee.

Design about Food is the design of objects inspired by food. Usually food as a material is not used in this category; instead, food is used to emphasize, reinterpret or inspire a product's message. Examples are all the various body products that smell, look and often feel like food: e.g. chocolate body cream, egg shaped bath salt, and popcorn soap. An interesting example is a line of T-shirts packaging designed by *Prompt:\Design*, for which the designers won a Gold Pentaward in 2010. (see Figure 5)

Another example of what could be called Design about Food is Eszter Imre's collection *Table-Wear*. (see Figure 6) The artist cuts, combines, and redesigns portions of ceramic tableware to create jewelry. Her intent with this collection is to bring people back to the old tea break where etiquette, status and appearance are at the essence of the eating experience. These objects are about bringing history back to life with delicately hand painted porcelain pieces, while at the same time elevating such objects to jewelry, giving them a completely different function, and an entirely new meaning. Eszter says that she wants to design things that are simple but with a little twist, objects that are unique and personal, objects that we trust and love. Being jewellery these pieces are not designed *for* food, but still are *about* food because they are inspired by food and because food consumption (i.e. drinking tea) is what they want to evoke.

Finally **Eating Design** is about the design of any eating situation where there are people interacting with food.

This is a very broad definition that explains that restaurant-eating situations, the ones that usually first come to mind, are only one option: eating situations can also be eating popcorn at the cinema, having a picnic in the park, eating a sandwich while walking to work, or any other situation which includes people and food, with no restriction to environment, companions and service (or absence of such).

An example of Eating Design that is not related to the restaurant environment and also shows how eating situations can range, is designed by the Eating Designer Marije Vogelzang - who is probably the most well known eating designer. In her book *Eat Love* she defines herself an eating designer, and not a food designer *because I'm not just focused on the aesthetics, I deliberately don't call myself a Food Designer but an Eating Designer. The food itself is already perfectly designed by nature, so there's hardly anything I have to add to it (p.73).* Determined to find a way to make her daughter eat vegetables she organized a Veggie Bling Bling party for her daughter and her friends; she then asked them to make jewelries using only their teeth as instruments. Without realizing it, and while having a lot of fun, her daughter ate carrots, tomatoes, lettuce, radish and much more (see Figure 7).

These different Food Design sub-categories show that Food Design is as diverse as the many disciplines that influence the design process and the design outcome. What is certain is that from whatever angle, Food Design has the potential to create products and services that are engaging, inspiring, surprising, fun and meaningful.

FOOD INSPIRES DESIGN

GRANDMA'S
APPLE PIE
WITH APRICOTS
INSPIRES
THE DESIGNER
TO CREATE
HOMEMADE/
HANDMADE

The Grandma

NAME
Rosa

COUNTRY
Belgium

RECIPE
Apple pie with apricots

ROSA

Rosa De Rijck is famous for her passion for desserts, not only in her family but also throughout the whole village of Schiplaken. She is the weekly baker for some local associations' meetings. She also makes dozens of apple pies for the annual Christmas market. She truly deserves the title of "baking grandma of Schiplaken". Her own children and grandchildren love most of her desserts, but their favourite is this apricot and apple pie. The pie has been the star at all of her grandchildren's birthday parties for the last twenty years. It's not only delicious but also perfect for putting little candles on top.

RECIPE > HISTORY AND TRADITION

This apple pie with apricots is a typical "farmer's pie". It's made with ingredients that have always been available on the farm or in the neighbourhood. Apples were found in the garden. Eggs came from the chickens and flour from the mill not far from the farm. People just baked with what they had. For the pie pastry, Rosa still uses her sixty-year-ago recipe.

APPLE PIE WITH APRICOT

INGREDIENTS

a 30 cm cake/tart mould
250g self-raising flour
80g sugar
150g butter
1 egg

For the vanilla cream:
750cl milk
4 tsp sugar
60g vanilla powder

For the filling:
6 apples
1 egg yolk

For the apricot coulis:
a 500cl can of apricots in syrup
1 tsp sugar
a little vanilla powder
1 1/2 tsp Grand Marnier

PREPARATION

The day before:
Start by making the tart dough. Sieve the flour on the table and make a hollow in the flour. Pour the sugar, butter and egg into the middle of the hollow. Knead the dough very thoroughly until it is smooth and elastic.
Cover the dough with tin foil. Place it in the fridge for one night.

The next morning:
Make the vanilla cream, the filling and the coullis.

The vanilla cream: Bring the milk and sugar to the boil. Thicken with the vanilla powder.
Heat the oven to 220°C. Grease the mould with butter and flour. Roll out the dough and place it in the mould. Pour the cream over the dough.

The filling: Peel and slice the apples. Arrange the apple slices on the pie. Brush with some egg. Place the pie in the oven at 220°C for 30-35 minutes, depending on the power of the oven.
Take the pie out of the oven, leave to cool and remove it from the mould.

The coulis: Mix all the ingredients, except the Grand Marnier. Heat it and allow to thicken. When it is ready, add the Grand Marnier. Pour it over the pie.
Leave the sauce to cool and serve the pie.

The Designer

NAME & COUNTRY
Amélia Desnoyers, France

EDUCATION
National Superior Diploma in Visual Arts from
the ENSBA (École Nationale Supérieure des
Beaux Arts de Paris); Certificate in
Professional Aptitude (CAP) in Pastry,
Contextual Master from the Design Academy
of Eindhoven

FIELD OF EXPERTISE
Culinary art, food experiences, porcelain collection
design for the Vista Alegre company in Portugal

WEBSITE
http://ameliadesnoyers.com

Dear Rosa,

would like to thank you for inspirin
th your Apple tart recipe and especially
u explained your experience of cooking.
really liked your way of cooking with wha
vailable around us. It made me reflect on
nsumption habits and how we have lost ou
atural habilities of making with our hands

The Concept

HOMEMADE/HANDMADE

CATEGORY

Design For Food (DFF)

DESCRIPTION

Rosa's typical farmer's pie is made with ingredients that have always been available on the farm or in the neighbourhood. To make her cakes, Rosa uses her hands and what she can find around her. This rolling pin made from a log of wood found in the farm illustrates how you can create your own crafted tools for cooking. It shows how a simple raw material, which can be found anywhere, is transformed into a useful traditional yet sophisticated tool. Its natural qualities perpetuate the traditional craft concepts of homemade and handmade food and objects.

THE FARMER'S PIE AND ITS CRAFTED ROLLING PIN

BY AMELIA DESNOYERS

Rosa 's typical farmer's pie is made with ingredients that have always been available on the farm or in the neighborhood.

Rosa bakes with her hands and uses what she finds around her to make her cakes.

This rolling pin made with a log of wood found in the farm illustrates how we can create our own crafted tools to cook.

It shows how a simple row material, which can be found anywhere, is transformed into a useful traditional yet sofisticated tool.

IT's natural qualities perpetuates the traditional concept of homemade / handmade food and objects related to crafts.

FOOD INSPIRES DESIGN

GRANDMA'S
SAMSA
INSPIRES
THE DESIGNER
TO CREATE
TATLY

The Grandma

CANAN

Canan Kutay learned how to make samsa from her father-in-law, who originated from Turkistan.
She chose to share the recipe of samsa because, like many ancient dishes, this one is being forgotten.
She thinks that it is rarely prepared in Istanbul households nowadays, because it is a time-consuming and difficult recipe. Samsa was a unique dessert prepared on special (religious) occasions to be offered to guests by her family.

RECIPE > HISTORY AND TRADITION

The word samsa originates from the Persian samôse/sambûse, meaning triangular-shaped pastry. Samsa has been present in Anatolia since the 14th Century and it is probably one of the pastry dishes that came to Anatolia with the Turkic tribes migrating from Central Asia. Semsek, a savoury variety of samsa is still made today in the southeastern region of Anatolia. Sweet samsa has formed a part of elite Istanbul cuisine since the Ottoman era. In an Ottoman cookbook published in the 19th Century (Housewife/ Ev Kadını, 1882), samsa is described as a kind of baklava soaked in syrup. It was also one of the desserts served in the Ottoman palace. For example, samsa appears on the menu of a banquet served on 3rd July 1913 in the Ottoman palace in honour of Sultan Resat. In today's classical Istanbul cuisine, samsa is a kind of flaky walnut-filled pastry soaked in syrup. However, some families originating from Central Asia, serve samsa without syrup.

SAMSA

INGREDIENTS

For the dough:
500g wheat flour
10g salt
70ml olive oil
200ml water
400g butter
15ml raisin vinegar
50ml olive oil

For the filling:
250g walnuts
2 tsp cinnamon
60g granulated sugar
1 tbsp water

For the coating and glaze:
icing sugar
1 egg yolk, lightly beaten

PREPARATION

The dough:
Combine the salt with the sifted flour. Make a hollow in the centre and add 70ml olive oil, water, vinegar and butter. Work these ingredients with your fingertips to make a creamy mixture and then mix in a circular motion, drawing in flour from the outside. Knead for about 10 or 15 minutes until the dough becomes very smooth and elastic. Fold the dough and cover it with plastic film. Chill for 30 minutes. Roll out the dough so that it is 20cm across and brush it with 50ml olive oil. Then fold it and place it in the refrigerator for another 30 minutes. Repeat this step 5 times. Meanwhile, prepare the filling.

The filling:
Mix the chopped walnuts, cinnamon and sugar with a small amount of water.

Coating and baking:
Once the dough is ready, divide it into 2 pieces. Roll out each piece to 30cm on a lightly floured surface. Divide the sheet of pastry into 9 squares and place 1 tablespoonful of walnut mixture inside each square. Then fold in the opposite corners. Place them on a tray and glaze with egg yolk. Bake in a preheated oven (175°C) for 25-30 minutes. Once the samsas are cooked, dust them with icing sugar and serve hot.

The Designer

NAME & COUNTRY
Claire Chuniaud, Tiphaine Rolland
and Claire Cheverry, France

EDUCATION
Graphic Design students at the School of Design
in Nantes, France, in the New Eating Habits
section.

FIELD OF EXPERTISE
Combining graphic design with cuisine

WEBSITE
http://chuniaudclaire.tumblr.com
http://www.behance.net/tiphainerolland

Dear Canan Kutay,

We would like to express all our gratitude for that beautiful discovery that you gave us. It allowed us to think differently about the tradition and the sharing of the samsa in your country. And what a sharing! By means of that video you offered us a special access to the Turkish culture as well as a unique knowhow. A learning process that we tried to transcribe again to our project. You not only revealed a delicious recipe, you also took us to your country, your family and your knowledge. We really appreciate that you showed us your garden. A little corner of paradise, so intimate, that opens to us. Preparing your samsa step by step, reminds us of our childhood when we admired our granny making us a cake. The final result of this video and this project: we have a haste and eat your samsa in a sweet floral garden in Turkey.

The Concept

TATLY

CATEGORY

Food Product Design (FPD)

DESCRIPTION

We developed our Tatly project based on Canan Kutay's samsa recipe. It serves as a gift to offer to someone to whom you wish to pass on knowledge or a tradition. It is also an invitation to travel, to discover a country and its cuisine.
Tatly is a half-finished product containing all the necessary ingredients to make two little cakes. We were inspired by the traditional tableware used by Canan Kutay in the video. Everything in the package encourages the use of the senses:
The eyesight is drawn to the glass through which the ingredients can be seen, it can be smelled, touch is required for the cooking and taste is needed to savour the finished product. Cooking is a moment of sharing and transmission, a gift.
Discover Turkey through Tatly.

Tatly

Research

Then we wanted to touch, smell, see and taste the food. So we worked on a trendy sheet and with photography to visually convey textures, tastes and even odours of various ingredients as Canan Kutay gave us the desire across the video. This work allowed us to highlight the raw material, the ingredients: pure, nude. We wished to keep this idea in our creation.

Inspirations

We have been inspired by the Turkish culture. In passing by the calligraphy, the jewelry, the embroidery, dervishes, the henna or even lamps, we have been impregnated by its universe. We can find heavy ornaments, elegant curves, warm and contrasting colours, a precious and ephemeral side. We have been touched by her garden and the attention she brings to her flowers. We wanted to smell and discover them.

Visual Identity

For this gift, we wanted a simple name, emotional and soft. We chose «Tatly», which is normally written «Tatlik», the diminutive of «Tatlik», «softness» in Turkish language. We matched it with a long, elegant and ornamented typeface like the Turkish calligraphy and its style. We put henna illustrations in the visual identity to reinforce the Turkish universe, just as the contrasted colours.

Sketches

And then we got the idea to create a present, a transmission of this recipe to a close person, a sharing, but also a little box to offer with which we could redo the cake. This product also highlights Turkish tradition and culture, as an invitation to travel. This is a jar which let us discover the food and its texture. As in the video, we already have the taste in the mouth, the odor that comes to us and we can

Our Grandma

Samsa

Canan Kutay

We have been touched by Canan Kutay who made us discover the Samsa from Turkey. These cakes are normally cooked for events, they ask a knowhow and a long preparation, especially for the dough. As this woman cooks we feel both the tradition and her pride. It is a dish which comes from her family and she brightly succeeds in doing it. Under the Turkish sun, in a flowered garden, we follow the steps of the Samsa's preparation. The tableware is in glass with typical ornaments, the creamy dough mixing until the delicious filling of the pastries she shares afterwards. We wish to convey, as she does, the values of tradition by the sharing of that cuisine.

GET READY TO COOK

BOTTOM

TOP

VERSO COVER PLATE

RECTO COVER PLATE

FIG SAMSAS

CORK

TEA BAGS

COVER PLATE

Concept

Tatfy's product is a gift or invitation to offer a close person, child, or to travel. This box contains the necessary ingredients to make a Turkish recipe, such as a samsa. The engraved glass jar refers to the traditional tableware. We observe the ingredients, see the textures and imagine the tastes and odours which make us elated as we look them. By opening the pot, we have the ingredients that make up the filling in a separated inner packaging for a healthy matter; and then the precut pastries. In the cork we discover a cover plate, decorated by a flower from the country. Thanks to scented polish, we can smell the flower by a friction of the picture, we are immersed in a Turkish garden. By removing the cover plate, we find on the reverse side the recipe of the cake. It is possible to keep the cardboard as a perfumed memory of a shared moment, but also to pass by the cake. We also have two tea bags in the cork because this is a typical drink from Turkish culture. We relay knowledge, but we also share a precious moment.

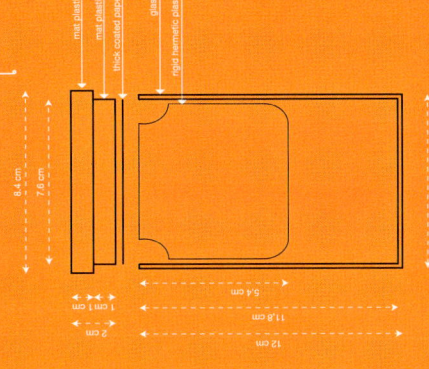

Claire Chuniaud - Tiphaine Rolland - Claire Cheverry

Technique

mat plastic
mat plastic
thick coated paper
glass
rigid hermetic plastic

8.4 cm
7.6 cm
2 cm
1 cm
1 cm
5/4 cm
11.8 cm
12 cm
8 cm

For the container that is also the packaging, we have used transparency with the help of a noble material, glass, which is reminiscent of Canan Kutay's tableware. To bring a traditional and custom side, we engraved the glass with Tatfy's logo. The cork is made of a matte plastic and lightly exceeds the jar's size to allow easier access. The cork is screwed with the help of walls in the glass for a hermetic closing. Inside the jar, we find a second container in rigid and hermetic transparent plastic to separate the ingredients from the pastry, which allows then user to remove the ingredients from the packaging properly. The cover plate which encloses the tea bags, is composed of thickly coated paper printed with scented ink, releasing a smell as the user touches the paper. Through our packaging, we wanted to induce four of the five senses: the sense of smell, vision, touch, and finally, the sense of taste.

FOOD
INSPIRES
DESIGN

GRANDMA'S
CASTAGNOLE
INSPIRES
THE DESIGNER
TO CREATE
GRANDMA
SERAFINA'S
CASTAGNOLES

The Grandma

NAME
Serafina

COUNTRY
Belgium

RECIPE
Castagnole

RECIPE > HISTORY AND TRADITION

In the 1950s many Italian workers came to Belgium. They found jobs in the car industry or in the mines in Limburg. Nowadays, the mines are closed but their descendants still live there. Many of them continue to make their Italian dishes in the traditional way. Castagnole is one such example from the dozens of Italian desserts. It originates from the Liguria, Emila and Lombardia regions. Nowadays, it is found all over Italy. They are most often made in February at carnival time.

CASTAGNOLE

INGREDIENTS

1kg flour
10 tsp sugar
3 sachets of vanilla sugar
2 sachets of baking powder
9 eggs
5 tsp Anici, an aniseed liqueur
10 tsp peanut oil

PREPARATION

Pour the flour into a bowl.
Add the sugar and the vanilla sugar. Mix well.
Sieve the baking powder into the bowl.
Make a hollow. Pour the eggs into the hollow one by one. Add the liqueur and the oil.
Mix well and knead until elastic and smooth.
Make little rolls of dough.
Deep-fry until gold brown.
Sprinkle with sugar and serve.

The Designer

NAME & COUNTRY
Roel Vandebeek, Belgium

EDUCATION
Roel Vandebeek finished his studies in
product design at the MAD Faculty
(Media, Arts & Design) in Genk, Belgium

FIELD OF EXPERTISE
All-round designer, active within different
subjects in the design world, founded his
own company, Beek Design in 1996

WEBSITE
www.beekdesign.be

an grandma Serafina,

hank you very much for your inspiring
cipe of Castagnoles.

rt by looking at them I wanted to
sign a customized packing because
ey deserve to be presented in a special way.

wish you all the best.

ind regards,

el Vandebeek

The Concept

GRANDMA SERAFINA'S CASTAGNOLES

CATEGORY

Design For Food (DFF)

DESCRIPTION

Grandma Serafina inspired me when she broke open the castagnole in the video. By doing so, she invites you to eat it. I translated this invitation into my exclusive packaging of the product. It's a new way of offering this homemade product with a lot of respect.

artisan

inviting

unfold

recycled paper

friendly

stackable

oil absorption

Grandma Serafina's Castagnoles

GRANDMA'S DESIGN

Design For Food
designer Roel Vandebeek

respecting baking tradition

hospitality

hand over

adjustable size

appreciation

artisan

inviting

unfold

recycled paper

friendly

stackable

oil absorption

FOOD
INSPIRES
DESIGN

GRANDMA'S
CINDERELLA
CAKE
INSPIRES
THE DESIGNER
TO CREATE
IPAD USER
RECIPE

The Grandma

NAME
Adriana

COUNTRY
Italy

RECIPE
Cinderella Cake

RECIPE > HISTORY AND TRADITION
Grandmother Adriana invented this cake and still bakes it a lot for her grandchildren. As they were used to her cake, they preferred to taste other ones during family lunches and on public holidays. That's why Adriana decided to make her cake more attractive: she called it 'Cinderella', after the fairytale. "Shall I bring Cinderella or not?" she asks her grandchildren now. And they all tell her to bring it.

The Recipe

CINDERELLA CAKE

INGREDIENTS

a round baking tin
500g flour
3 Reinette apples
50g melted butter
1/2 glass of oil
a pinch of salt
nuts, 50g of each: Almonds, hazelnuts, and walnuts
70g dark chocolate, broken into small pieces
grated rind of one lemon
100g sugar
4 eggs
1/2 glass of milk
1 packet of yeast

PREPARATION

Cut the apples into small pieces and place them in a
bowl. Add the flour to stop the apples from browning
and add the melted butter. Next add the oil, a pinch of
salt, the nuts, chocolate, grated lemon rind and sugar.
Mix the batter.
Heat the oven to 180°C.
Break the eggs into a bowl and whisk. When they are
whipped, add the batter and mix well.
Just before placing the cake into the oven, dissolve the
yeast in the milk, add it to the batter and mix it all
together well.
Grease the tin, pour the cake mixture into it and cook
at 180° C for about 40 minutes.

The Designer

NAME & COUNTRY
Sofia Badaoui, Anne-Axelle Bouilly
& Marie Visonneau, France

EDUCATION
First year students, Master in the New Eating
Habits section from L'École de Design Nantes
Atlantique based in Nantes, France

WEBSITE
http://www.sofiabadaoui.com
http://www.aabouilly.com
http://turing.lecolededesign.com/mvisonneau

Dear Adriana,

We are three French students who participated to Grandma's design competition. First of all, we would like to express our gratitude. Your recipe inspired us to make a great concept "The recipe of the use of iPad". As you mention in your video, you like computers but you don't understand them. Like you decided to teach us how to prepare your recipe, we decided to make you a recipe that enables you to understand new technologies. A recipe that helps you to use those new technologies in an independant way. The purpose of our concept is to explain how to use an iPad in several stages, with simple terms that explain you everything.

For instance, for young people the term "to zoom" is connected to a certain body movement on a touch sensitive screen, for an elderly person however it might have a different meaning. Our "recipe book" will allow an apprenticeship. The first stage will be to learn

The Concept

IPAD USER RECIPE

CATEGORY

Design About Food (DAF)

DESCRIPTION

We chose to work on Adriana's video of an Italian grandmother making a Cinderella cake. We watched the video many times and were struck by some key elements. Adriana speaks a lot about her past (her childhood, the war...). It seems to be really important to her and she wants to share it with us. When we replayed video, we noticed that she is very organised. All the ingredients she needed were set out in advance. We also noticed that she demonstrates all the cunning tricks of the preparation and reveals the importance of this cake in her life. She takes a lot of time to bake her cake that is now loved by her grandchildren. Indeed, she called it 'Cinderella cake' in order to make them appreciate it. We can feel her desire to make it popular and to enable other people to discover her recipe. And why not through the Web? In fact, she says that she loves computers, but she doesn't understand them. Considering all of these elements, we became interested in the idea of 'heritage'. At the beginning of her story this lady confesses that she is 89 years old. Her expression shows us that she can't believe it either. Furthermore, from her organised manner and the way she explains how to bake her cake we get the feeling that she wants to leave a 'footprint' of it once and for all. She wants other people to take advantage of her knowledge. By taking part in the competition, she emphasises this idea of 'heritage', the wish to pass the torch on to the next generation. So, the video is the source of the 'footprint', the interview is the footprint put into words and the recipe has been written down for future generations!

All of this because Adriana has understood something important: Young people will be more interested in grandmother's recipes if they are broadcast on Youtube: The place to be for the new generation. Therefore, we have retained this idea of sharing heritage. And the fact that Adriana likes computers developed our concept: "The iPad user recipe".

CAKE WITH
Hands

INGREDIENTS

- 1 iPad
- 2 beautiful index fingers
- 100gr of concentration
- a pinch of will

LEVEL

TIME

1 Briefly touch the screen with your index finger. *This action allows to select a component as to open an app.*

2 Touch quickly two times the screen with your index finger. *This action allows to enlarge a picture.*

3 Touch a long time with your index finger. *This action allows to save, to copy or delete a component.*

4 Put your index finger on the right of the screen and slide it on the left without take it off. *This action allows to change the page or a picture likes the pages of a book.*

5 Put your index fingers stick together and take them away one from the other without take them off. *This action allows to enlarge a picture.*

6 Put your index fingers far one from the other and gather them together. *This action allows to reduce a picture.*

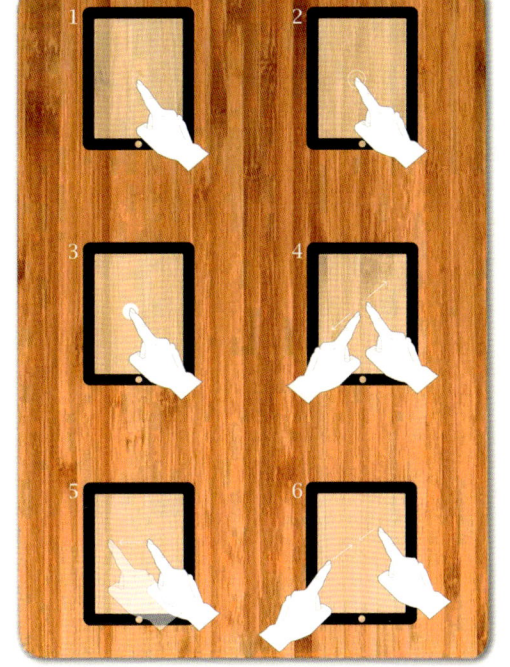

THE GRAND MOTHER

ADRIANA / 89 YEARS OLD

«Now I like computers, I don't understand them very well but (...) I'm curious about them!»

Adriana uses a computer to learn us how to make her cake, so we will use a recipe to learn her how to use an iPad. In this way, the elderly are going to be able to confront themselves with the new technologies in a playful and simple way.

CREATIVE APPROACH

At the beginning, this lady confess that she is 89 years old. Her expression showed us that she couldn't believe it too. Furthermore, all the organization and her way to explain how to cook her cake (she gives some tricks) give us the feeling that she want to let a « track » of it once and for all. She wants that other people take advantages of her knowledges. By participate to this competition, she emphasizes this idea of « heritage », the wish to pass on the torch to the next generation. Then, the video is the importance of the « track ». The interview is the track by the words and the recipe is written for young people ! All of this because Adriana understands something important : Young people will be more interested by grand-mother's recipe if they are broadcast on Youtube : the place of passage for all the new generation. Therefore we retained this idea of sharing, heritage and the fact that Adriana likes computers develop our concept.

THE RECIPE
OF
User guide

THE CONCEPT

THE RECIPE OF USER GUIDE

Retranscribe cooking's appropriate codes by passing down knowledges like in cookbooks but in an inappropriate way: for iPad.

The purpose is to explain how to use an iPad in several stages, with simple terms which are going to speak to the elderly. Indeed, if for us the term «to zoom» is connected to a certain body movements on a touch-sensitive screen, it's not the same thing for an elderly person. Our «book of recipe» will allow a apprenticeship stage by stage, every recipe (takings) representing a new stage of the apprenticeship. The first stage will be to learnt them the body movements (to zoom, to click, to copy and paste etc.), and the second will be to use the applications of bases of an iPad and so forth.

The choice of the iPad is not harmless, after some researches we were able to notice that the manipulation of the iPad is simpler than using a computer. Indeed, it does not require a connection specific which can annoy the elderly. Furthermore, its use is more intuitive. We are going to touch it with our fingers by selecting the element wanted, the same way we touch the food that we cook.

CAKE WITH Hands

INGREDIENTS

1 iPad

2 beautiful index fingers

100gr of concentration

a pinch of will

1 Briefly touch the screen with your index finger. *This action allows to select a component as to open an app.*

2 Touch quickly two times the screen with your index finger. *This action allows to enlarge a picture.*

3 Touch a long time with your index finger. *This action allows to save, to copy or delete a component.*

4 Put your index finger on the right of the screen and slide it on the left without take it off. *This action allows to change the page or a picture likes the pages of a book.*

5 Put your index fingers stick together and take them away one from the other without take them off. *This action allows to enlarge a picture.*

6 Put your index fingers far one from the other and gather them together. *This action allows to reduce a picture.*

FOOD INSPIRES DESIGN

GRANDMA'S
KARELIAN PIES
INSPIRES
THE DESIGNER
TO CREATE
KRUISP

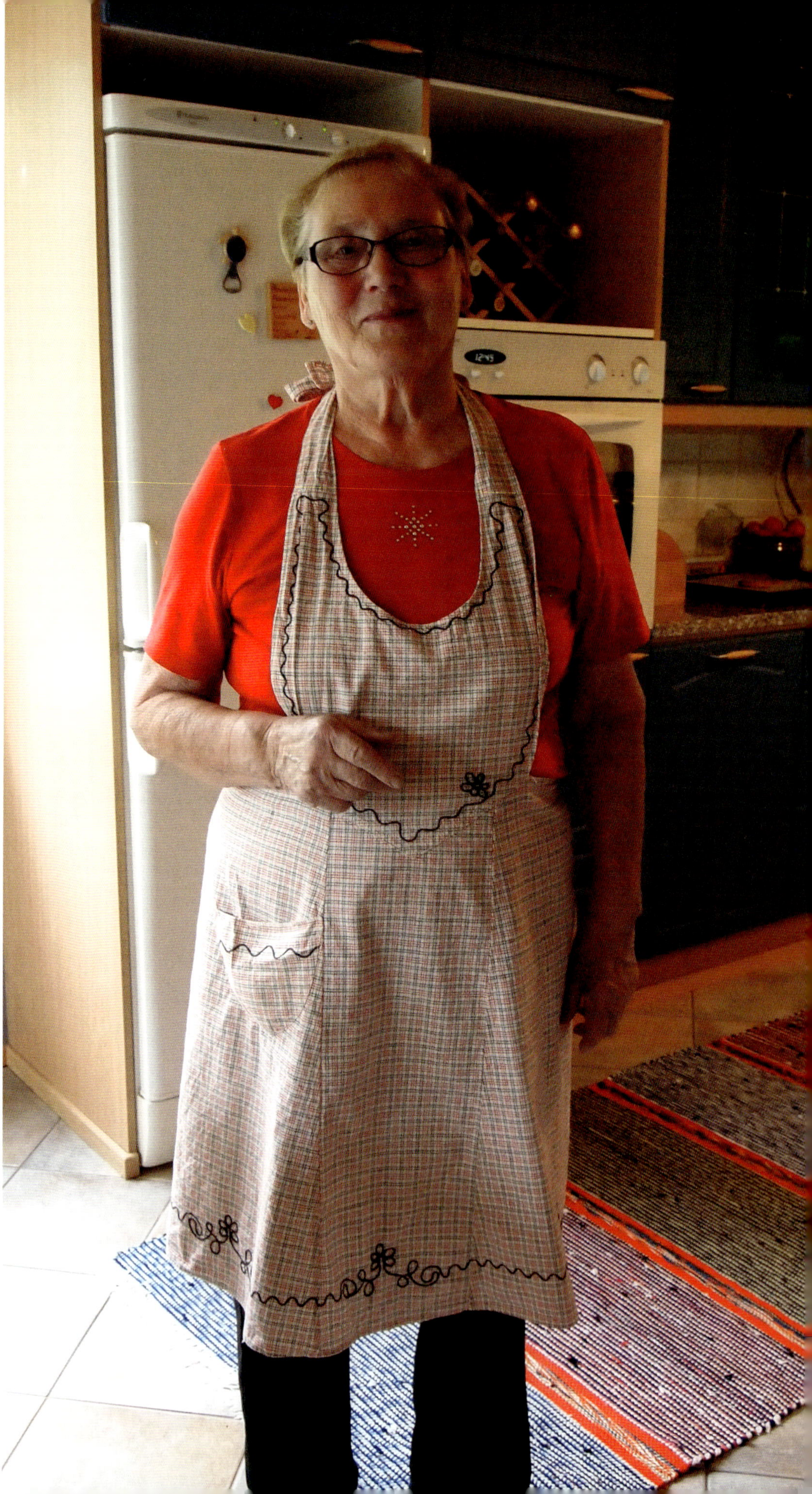

The Grandma

NAME
Liisa

COUNTRY
Finland

RECIPE
Karelien Pies

RECIPE > HISTORY AND TRADITION

Originally, Karelian pies or karjalanpiirakka were baked in Finnish Northern Karelia and the Ladogan Karelia and Border Karelia regions, which were lost to Russia in World War II. During and after the war, inhabitants from the lost Karelia were re-housed all over Finland, spreading the tradition throughout the country. The dough was originally made using rye flour. When wheat became more common in Karelia, wheat flour was mixed with the rye. The only other ingredients used are water and salt. The dough is rolled into oval pies using a special rolling pin and filled with barley, rice or potato porridge. The dough is gathered around the filling covering the edges, but leaving it open in the middle. The pies are baked in a very hot oven and served as a snack with egg butter and coffee.

KARELIAN PIES

INGREDIENTS

For the rice porridge/filling:
200ml water
200g rice
1l milk
1 tsp salt
a dash of cream
1 egg

For the dough:
200ml water
a handful wheat flour
a handful rye flour
2 tbsp oil
1 tsp salt

PREPARATION

The rice porridge: Prepare the rice porridge well in advance so it may cool down. Bring the water to the boil, add the rice and cook until the water is absorbed. Add the milk and let it simmer. Add the cream and season with salt.

The dough: Mix the ingredients and knead into a firm dough. Roll the dough about 1cm thick. Cut into round cakes with a glass. Roll each piece into a thin round crust.

Beat the egg into the cooled rice porridge until incorporated.
Fill the centre of each crust with a thin layer of rice porridge and smooth it down a bit. Fold the edges of the crusts and pinch tightly with your fingers to form oval-shaped pies.
Bake on a baking sheet at 300°C for 15 minutes.
Brush with a mixture of butter and water.
Cover with a kitchen towel.

The Designer

NAME & COUNTRY
Federico Poggioli, Italy
and Joanne Lin, Singapore

EDUCATION
Both: Masters in Industrial
and Strategic Design at Aalto
University School of Arts, Design
and Architecture;
Federico: BA degree from the Politecnico
di Milano; Joanne, BA from the National
University of Singapore

FIELD OF EXPERTISE
Food cultures, art and design

WEBSITE
http://joannelin.wordpress.com

KIITOS
MUMMO
LIISA!!!

While making it, we felt that the simple crust with the
thy rye actually makes it a good base for other types of fillings.
started experimenting with other types of porridges found in our
he countries (Italialainen ja Singaporelainen) and realised that
makes these recipes become easy to eat snacks that look
eautiful at the same time.

We hope you might be interested to try our recipes as
nd experiment with other fillings because the Karelian pie crust is
...ld make a new flavour that is very

The Concept

KRUISP

CATEGORY

Design With Food (DWF)

DESCRIPTION

Our concept is called KRUISP (K for Karelian, RUIS meaning rye and P for Pie). We describe it as a pie of Finnish design with a multicultural filling. Karelian pie is a traditional Finnish recipe and the filling can be of different cultural origins while using the same crust. Thus, we create modular food with a cross-cultural flavour.

What started as a social commentary and exploration into traditional food led to the rediscovery of an unpretentious but smart Finnish (food) design. Our concept definitely reflects our constant questioning of the role of design at this point in time, when there is often a tension between creating something tangible and something essential.

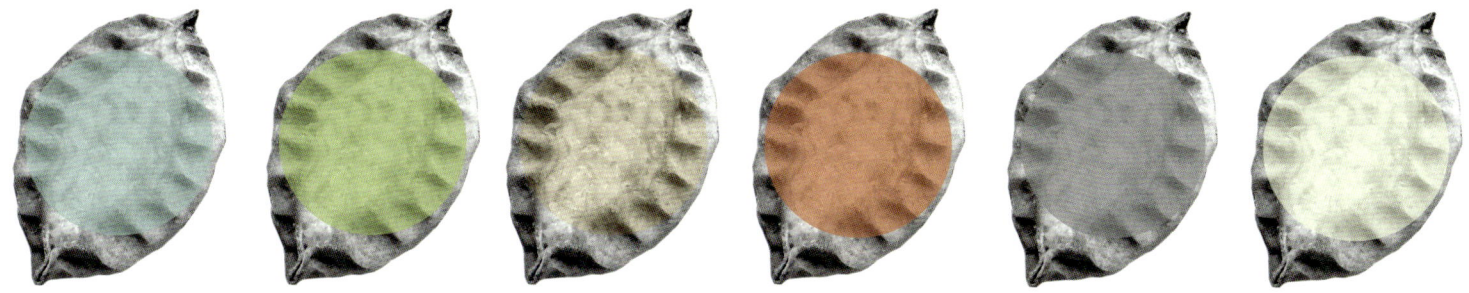

the democratic filling of finnish design

KRUISP

KARELIAN PIE
a finnish archetype

Federico Poggioli and Joanne Lin met in Finland in 2009 while studying Design at Aalto University School of Arts, Design and Architecture. Food, art, design and a bit of swimming were common grounds which they bonded over and became close friends. It was fitting that they finally came together to attempt a food design project with a reflective piece on Finland's food culture. What started as a social commentary and exploration into traditional food became a rediscovery of an unassuming but smart Finnish (food) design.

We chose mummo Liisa's Karelian Pie recipe because we felt there was something visually iconic yet surprisingly bland about it. As a carbo snack and a fresh treat from the oven with egg butter, the Karelian Pie was definitely a more appealing quick fix compared to a plain piece of bread; but even bread has its variations and tastier versions, but why not the Karelian pie? Well, you can find some variations but they always remained in the subtle flavour zone as compared to the robust and hearty flavours when we think of pies.

We then wondered about the notion of having a 'Traditional Specialty Guaranteed (TSG)' status in Europe, does it mean the recipe cannot be changed or it will lose its traditional authenticity? Through further investigation, we found out that the Karelian Pie did evolve overtime due to the various grains made available through trade and new cultures coming into Finland:

THE DEMOCRATIC FILLING
the concept

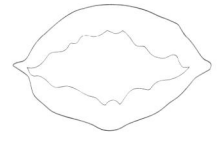

Finnish citizenships granted
Source: Statistics Finland, Demographic statistics

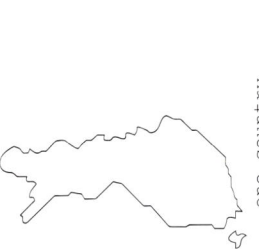

Russia	
Others	
Serbia & Montenegro	
Iran	
Turkey	
Sweden	
Estonia	
Afghanistan	
Somalia	
Iraq	
Ukraine	

The questions that came to mind with regard to baking traditions were therefore:

- What does it mean to revive and revitalise traditional food/recipes?
- How do we do it while retaining the authenticity of the recipe and it's symbolic linkages?
- What do we think about when we make such food?

And so we went to deconstruct the pie by constructing it, basically we went to cook; because like in design, knowing your materials can reveal to you design opportunities and answers.

one country   one crust

increasing   single filling
multi-culturalism

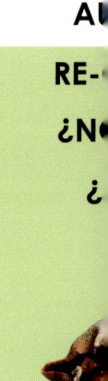

KARELIAN PIE
MEETS
ITALY

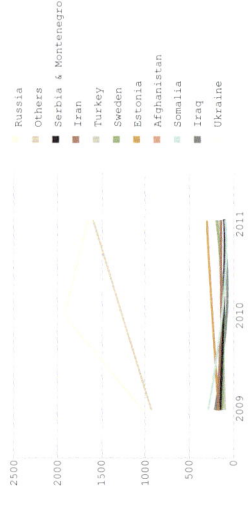

AU
RE-
¿NO
¿

barley   talkunna

welcoming
multi flavours

**modular food for cross cultural taste
same crust, different content**

tradition
evolution

?

While we were in Finland, it's population saw a steady rise of new citizens from different countries. Globally, human movement is inevitable and many capitals are in fact becoming vibrant melting pots of culture and activities. For some, these changes can be seen as a threat and erosion to the local ethnicity and identity of a place. One might begin to wonder if the constant mulling over preservation of tradition and heritage is a reaction to such occurrences than just a conscientious effort to remind the future of the past and it's lessons learnt.

While I was in Finland I always wondered why Karelian pies don't have different flavors / distinct ingredients from others. I decided to make a version with left over porcini risotto; where porcini is not only a really common ingredient but also really loved by italian people. In Italy, we have a big tradition with risotto, where everybody does in their own way. It's something personal. It's like pasta, where everyone has a sauce of their own that has.

K -(arelian)+
RUIS(rye) +
P -(ie) =
K R U I S P

Porridge is a common dish in Asia especially for those from the Chinese race. It is usually watery or smooth in texture and savoury in taste. One can eat it as a main meal with lots of ingredients or plain with other dishes like when eating rice. (Chinese) spinach and garlic are a typical vegetable-combo, whilst white pepper and sesame oil a common seasoning used when cooking Chinese dishes. When we were kids, our parents and grandparents used to cook us spinach porridge for us with meat or fish because it is thought to be very nutritious; strangely when one has grown up, the dish no longer appears. You'll hardly find it sold outside as well. It is truly a humble but special dish connected to memories, Asian roots and home cooking.

A SHELTER FOR TRADITION
for granted to forefront

Through this design attempt and exploration, we realised the solution wasn't always about change and new creations, but about recognition and rediscovery. In this case, the answer to revival was to take something for granted to the forefront!

We believe that the Karelian Pie crust has the potential to be a popular archetype for pie design. Bringing this pie design to the forefront not only revitalises it's status but also allows more people to know more about Finnish cuisine and be motivated to experiment with its versatile form.

We present to the world stage, a lesser known Finnish design, the Karelian Pie crust!

KARELIAN PIE
MEETS
SINGAPORE

OUR CULTURAL FILLING
an exploration

traditional version

100g short grain rice
500ml milk
100ml water
1/2 tsp salt
1/2 tsp cream
1/2 egg

chinese version

150g shrimp
150g spinach
100g short grain rice
5 small cloves of garlic
500ml water
50ml water (to pre-cook spinach)
1/2 tsp salt
1/2 tsp sesame oil
1/4 tsp white pepper
1 tsp oil (to pre-cook shrimp)

italian version

300g porcini mushrooms
100g short grain rice
1 clove of garlic
500ml water
50ml water
1/2 tsp salt
1/2 tsp olive oil
1/4 tsp parsley

CONSISTENCY
During the making and experimenting process, we realised the pasty consistency of the filling had an important role to play. How the filling came to be in the original recipe allowing the crimped edges to hold it's form by sticking a little to the filling is indeed fascinating.

CRUST
While using our cultures to attempt an authentic update of the Karelian Pie, it became evident that the crust was the most important in the fusion process. Although we started off initially with the filling, by embedding social commentary with regard to tradition and growing cultural influences; it started to dawn on us that the balance between tradition and vitality of the Karelian Pie actually lay in the crust. This is because the crust, with its strong design and composition, managed to capture the originality and locality of tradition perfectly. Its modularity was not just a versatile shell for contextually rich filling, it was the embodiment of contextually rich roots.

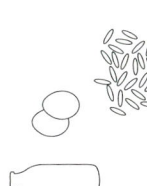

100 ml water
120g wheat flour
120g rye flour
1 tbs oil
1/2 tsp salt

FORM

Simple and fast (15 minutes baking) to make.

Smart design holds filling well while looking beautiful at the same time.

Requires filling that is sticky or pasty in nature.

Iconic and recognisable even when modified.

FUNCTION

Offers a modular shell to attempt authentic fusion creations.

Transforms pasty-like food into convenient finger food.

A great solution for leftovers!

HEALTH

Contains nutritious rye flour and olive oil.

A healthier alternative to fatty and oily pastry doughs and refined flour.

FOOD
INSPIRES
DESIGN

GRANDMA'S
BOJO
INSPIRES
THE DESIGNER
TO CREATE
BOJO CAKE-TAIL

The Grandma

NAME
Lucia

COUNTRY
the Netherlands

RECIPE
Bojo

LUCIA

Lucia was born in Suriname and grew up with this bojo cake. Bojo is the most common celebration recipe from Suriname.

RECIPE > HISTORY AND TRADITION

Bojo is a typical Suriname cake made of cassava and coconut. A party is not complete without a bojo. The bojo originates from the slave period and was created by the Creole people. The Creole culture is a fusion of diverse African, Indian and European cultures. Suriname was a colony of the Netherlands in 1667. Since 1975, Suriname is completely independent. Cassava is a versatile tuber, used as a main ingredient in dishes, as a side dish, in soups but also in sweet recipes. After the discovery of America, the Portuguese brought cassava to Africa and Asia. Nowadays cassava is an important food source for hundreds of millions of people.

BOJO

INGREDIENTS

2 tins
1kg cassava (ground)
250g coconut (grated)
$2^{1/2}$l coconut milk
250g margarine (melted)
2-3g salt
250g raisins (soaked)
1-2 tsp cinnamon
2 tsp vanilla essence
2 tsp almond essence
sugar (depends on your own taste)
some extra margarine (to grease the tins)
coloured speckles

PREPARATION

Heat the oven to 200°C and grease the tins.
Mix the cassava and coconut. Add the coconut milk
and mix it well together. Add the margarine (leaving
3 or 4 tbsp) and salt and mix. Then add all the raisins,
the cinnamon, vanilla essence and almond essence and
mix again. Add sugar to your own taste and mix it all
well together.
Spread the batter over the 2 tins. Drizzle with some
melted margarine and place in the middle of the oven
for 90 minutes.
Check regularly if the Bojo is cooked inside.
When the Bojo is ready, leave it to cool in its tin.
Sprinkle some coloured speckles on the top of each
Bojo and it's ready to eat!

The Designer

NAME & COUNTRY
Karla Rosales, the Netherlands

EDUCATION
Master in Design for Interaction at the TUDelft

FIELD OF EXPERTISE
Designing valuable user experiences that can connect people, technologists and companies regardless of the industry sector

WEBSITE
http://karlarosales.com

DEAR GRANDMA LUCIA & GRANDPA ROBBIE:

I am Karla and I chose your recipe for the Grandma's Design project. I was charmed by how you explained how to prepare a Bojo Cake. Based on your video I designed two concepts out of Bojo.

For my first design concept I designed a cocktail made with traditional dutch "jonge jenever" (young genever) infused with vanilla and coconut rum. It is garnished with grated cassava, nonpareils mixed with sugar and almond essence. I called it The Bojo Cake-tail. I found in my research that Bojo is used in birthdays and other celebrations. So I though to give it a more mature personality "A party is not complete without a bojo" right?

My second design concept is inspired in the typical common breakfast in the Netherlands. An Bojo Plakjes consist in two thin slices that combined together with bread and butter bring the flavour of the Bojo Cake for breakfast. One of the slices combines cassava, raisins and almonds while the other have vanilla, coconut and sweet Nonpareils.

Dutch culinary tradition has been enriched with the influences of its former colonies. My main objective was to celebrate the Surinamese influence in Dutch Culture through Bojo-inspired designs.

Thank you for inspiring me to reinterpret the Bojo-Cake. And I hope you liked my work.

GRAN TANGI!!!

Karla Rosales

The Concept

BOJO CAKE-TAIL

CATEGORY

Design With Food (DWF)

DESCRIPTION

The bojo cake-tail is the perfect companion for a party with friends. It has a bittersweet flavour that is both mellow and bold.
The bojo cake-tail is a cocktail made with traditional jonge jenever (young genever) infused with vanilla and coconut rum.
It is garnished with grated cassava, nonpareils mixed with sugar and almond essence.
We more often speak about the influence of the imperial nation in the former colonies. It is important to consider how it can work the other way around. Dutch culinary tradition has also been enriched with the influences of its former colonies.
The Bojo cake-tail is a celebration of the Surinamese influence on Dutch Culture.

BOJO
CAKE-TAIL

Most of the times we talk about the influence of the imperial nation in the former colonies. It is important to consider how it is the other way around. Dutch culinary tradition has been enriched with the influences of its former colonies. The Bojo Cake-tail is a celebration of the Surinamese influence in Dutch Culture.

Name: Karla Rosales
Country: The Netherlands
Grandma Lucia & Grandpa Robbie
Category: Designing with Food

Bojo cake-tail

DRINK INGREDIENTS:
2 SHOT VANILLA INFUSED DUTCH GENEVER
1 SHOT OF COCONUT RUM

CANDY/MIXER DECOR:
GRATED CASSAVA
COLOURFULL NONPAREILS
ALMOND ESSENCE

TOOLS:
BAR SPOON, SHAKER, ICE CUBES & MARTINI GLASS.

DESCRIPTION:
BECAUSE "A PARTY IS NOT COMPLETE WITHOUT A BOJO". THE **BOJO CAKE-TAIL** IS THE PERFECT COMPANION WHEN PARTYING WITH FRIENDS. IT POSSESSES A BITTERSWEET FLAVOR THAT IS MELLOW AND BOLD.

THE **BOJO CAKE-TAIL** IS A COCKTAIL MADE WITH TRADITIONAL "JONGE JENEVER" (YOUNG GENEVER) INFUSED WITH VANILLA AND COCONUT RUM. IT IS GARNISHED WITH GRATED CASSAVA, NONPAREILS MIXED WITH SUGAR AND ALMOND ESSENCE.

FOOD INSPIRES DESIGN

GRANDMA'S
SNOWSTAR
INSPIRES
THE DESIGNER
TO CREATE
SERVING SWEET
MAGIC

The Grandma

NAME
Annie

COUNTRY
the Netherlands

RECIPE
Snowstar

RECIPE > HISTORY AND TRADITION
The name of the pie is 'sneeuwster' (' snowstar') because it looks like a snow star. The cake consists in a soft sponge with a layer of eggnog and whipped cream in between. You can fill it with anything you like and it will taste good. The top is cut into 12 slices. After the eggnog and the whipped cream, the slices are placed on top to form a star. The icing sugar imitates snow and it really looks like a delicious soft snow star.

SNOWSTAR

INGREDIENTS

a round baking tin
4 eggs
1 tbsp vanilla sugar
150g sugar
1 $^{1/2}$ tbsp water
125g flour
45g cornstarch
 1/2 tsp baking powder
500ml cream
7 tbsp sugar
 1/2 tsp salt
200ml eggnog
icing sugar

PREPARATION

Heat the oven to 150°C and grease a tin.
Beat the eggs in a bowl with a mixer. Add the vanilla sugar, sugar and water and beat this mixture gently for 10-15 minutes. Mix the flour, cornstarch and baking powder and add it to the batter.
Put the batter in a round baking tin and bake it for 45 minutes in the oven.
Cool the pie for 10 minutes and remove it from the oven. Remove the pie from the tin.
Halve the pie horizontally and cut the upper layer in 12 pieces.
Mix the cream with 7 tbsp sugar and the salt; beat it until stiff.
Spread the eggnog over the lower part of the pie and cover it with cream, from the middle with a point to the outside. Arrange the 12 pieces on the cream. Dust the pie with icing sugar.
Put the snowstar in the fridge for a couple of hours.

The Designer

NAME & COUNTRY
Ana Maria Jimenez Amaro,
Spain

EDUCATION
Graphic Designer and Graphic Editor since
2008 and Industrial Designer since 2011

FIELD OF EXPERTISE
Food design, combining design studies
with gastronomic fusion

CONTACT
nika_jim@hotmail.com

Dear Grandmother Annie!
I chose your cake because inside
the sponge, cream, sugar cake I
could see a world of sweetness,
delicacy, innocense and magic.

It's not only for the ingredients
but also for the message I
received from you when you made
the cake.

Thanks for all Annie!

Ana.

The Concept

SERVING SWEET MAGIC

CATEGORY
Design With Food (DWF)

DESCRIPTION
I've always said that good things come in small portions. But if as well as being sweet experiences, they carry you through colours, smells and design, then they become something special. The snow star dessert was redesigned based on these factors, transforming it into something magical and interactive for the user.

SNOW STAR

HAPPINESS is inside OF A *sweet* & *magical* **WORLD**

sugar sphere

whipped cream, but not

more cake!

hot white chocolate syrup

tender
sponge
cake

roast milk
eggnog

icing
sugar
snow

One day, when i was little my grandmother gave me a crystal ball the sensation of feeling a new and magical world in my hands was fabulous.

The longing and innocence of my childhood are transmitted from snowstar. Where the colors and smells are merged in different textures and make the act of eating is a reliving a childhood experience.

BREAK THE SHELL AND DIVE INTO YOUR WORLD!

FOOD INSPIRES DESIGN

GRANDMA'S
FLEMISH WAFFLES
INSPIRES
THE DESIGNERS
TO CREATE
SUGAR SPRINKLER
AND
DECONSTRUCTED
BENEDICT

The Grandma

NAME
Goedele

COUNTRY
Belgium

RECIPE
Flemish Waffles

GOEDELE

Goedele presents us with a family recipe, handed down from one generation to the next. The huge textile crisis in West-Vlaanderen forced Goedele's grandmother to relocate to Asse. Goedele still follows her grandmother's recipe and almost every month the much loved waffles make their appearance on the menu.

RECIPE > HISTORY AND TRADITION

Although you see them everywhere in Belgium, waffles are not a Belgian invention. In the Middle Ages they could already be found in Paris. In old history books they are also mentioned in the Netherlands and Germany. We read of 'waffle street vendors' for the first time in the 17th Century. The famous Brussels waffle is first mentioned at the end of the 19th Century. After that, many restaurants specialised in waffles appeared. It was at that point that the waffle became famous and popular in Belgium. People love waffles for their taste, but also because they do not require many ingredients and they are fairly cheap to make. The most famous type is the Brussels waffle. There are also Flemish waffles, which are similar. The main difference is the size; the shape and the ingredients are the same.

FLEMISH WAFFLES

INGREDIENTS

a waffle iron
1kg flour
1l milk
1/2l water
50g yeast
400g butter
2 sachets vanilla sugar
pinch of salt
10 eggs

PREPARATION

Pour the flour into a very large bowl.
Make a hollow and pour the liquids into it.
Crumble the yeast into the liquid. Add the melted butter.
Next, add the vanilla sugar. Finish by adding the salt
and the egg yolks.
Whisk the egg whites. Gently fold them into the batter
using a spatula.
Leave the batter to rise in a warm place for at least
two hours. Be sure that your bowl is large enough!
Bake the waffles in a waffle iron.

The Designer

NAME & COUNTRY
Kyung Lim,
United Kingdom

EDUCATION
Last term student at Le Cordon Bleu, London

FIELD OF EXPERTISE
Food and travel

WEBSITE
http://kyums.com

Dear Goedele,

Thank you, from the bottom of my heart, for sharing your recipe, which was a delicious inspiration for my own design! Even though I am not from Belgium, I can relate to the joy that you feel when sharing waffles or other delicious goodies with your family, friends, and neighbors, and I wanted to create something similar. Besides, my husband is from Belgium, and I seem to have absorbed the taste for waffles and pastries from him!

I wanted to combine your recipe with breakfast, my favorite meal of the day. However, now I faced a dilemma: some people, myself included, prefer to have a light and sweet breakfast. Other people (my husband comes to mind) crave hearty food, like eggs and strips of bacon. In the end, I simply decided to combine both, and I used your recipe - literally - as the base for my concept. On a waffle made according to your recipe I placed an "egg" made from tofu cheesecake, which sits atop a layer of dried orange juice, to create the impression of bacon.

I hope that this recipe will make everybody happy, and I thank you, not just for sharing your recipe with me, but also for showing me that good food is so much better when you share it with the people you love.

Sincerely,

Kyung Lim

The Concept

DECONSTRUCTED BENEDICT

CATEGORY

Design With Food (DWF)

DESCRIPTION

For my Easter breakfast, I wanted it all: Something buttery, something sweet and a daily portion of fruit, all in one sitting. I started with my favourite savoury breakfast, the classic Eggs Benedict, and deconstructed it into a 'dessert in disguise'. Goedele's waffle recipe forms the base layer for this breakfast. Wild honeycomb candy, made with honey, syrup and baking soda, forms the second layer. The baking soda helps to release carbon dioxide bubbles that create layers and holes mimicking honeycomb. The honeycomb candy is covered with a thin layer of orange taffy, made from dehydrated orange juice that I reduced overnight. The result is a tart and zesty orange flavoured layer. On top sits an oval shaped tofu cheesecake, moulded by resourcefully using an eggshell to simulate a poached egg. By using tofu, the result is a savoury cheesecake, which is low in calories without compromising flavour. Lastly, I added a drizzle of custard to make the dish buttery and complete. For the entire recipe I used simple ingredients that can be found in any kitchen.

deconstructed

benedict

benedict

deconstructed

CREME ANGLAISE

COCONUT MILK, EGG YOLK, SUGAR, VA-

NILLA POD

TOFU CHEESECAKE MOLDED IN EGG SHELL

TOFU, CREAM CHEESE, ORANGE JUICE, HEAVY CREAM, GELATIN, SUGAR, VANILLA POD

DEHYDRATED FRUIT ROLL

ORANGE JUICE

HONEYCOMB CANDY

HONEY, CORN SYRUP, BAKING SODA

FLEMISH WAFFLES : GRANDMA GOEDELE'S RECIPE

FLOUR, YEAST, VANILLA SUGAR, BUTTER, MILK, WATER, SALT, EGGS

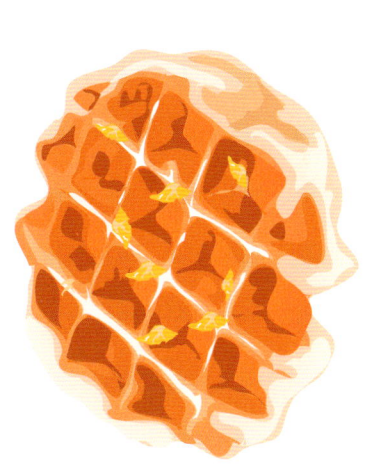

The Designer

NAME & COUNTRY
Caroline Dobbs, Belgium

EDUCATION
Higher Art Education: Sint Lucas Paviljoen,
Antwerp, Master in jewellery design
and goldsmith
Higher Education in the Arts: IKA Mechelen,
Glass Art Work

CONTACT
caroline.dobbs@skynet.be

Dear Goedele,

Thank you for presenting your Flemish waffles recipe
to the Grandma's Design project.

I have participated in this project because the initiative
seems fun and I enjoy creating new designs
for old uses.

After seeing almost all entries I decided to continue
with yours because it inspired me the most.

I have designed a waffle iron and a sugar caster.
The waffle maker bakes waffles in the shape of a styl-
ized flower. I drew a second set of irons to put some variety on the plate. The sugar caster sprinkles icing
sugar in that same flower shape.

Thanks again for your cooperation.

My best regards,
Caroline Dobbs

The Concept

SUGAR SPRINKLER

CATEGORY

Design For Food (DFF)

DESCRIPTION

The sugar sprinkler has three separate compartments in it for holding three different colours of icing sugar. At the bottom there is a wire mesh with a cut out stylised flower. By turning the coloured part at the bottom, the three different colours of sugar are sprinkled together to produce a lovely flower pattern.

Nature has been a source of inspiration for centuries. Her boundless diversity, elusive vastness and sheer beauty have captivated me. By intuitively combining carefully selected materials and aligning them with the fascinating process that melts sand into glass, the meticulously blown hot liquid glass is brought to life. With natural, geometric shapes and subtle yet powerful lines governed by harmony, I strive to produce uncomplicated designs, which are carefully thought out yet also dynamic!

Goedeles sugar caster

4 soft flavoured types of icing sugar

choose your own favourite flavour!

Vanilla

Orange

Raspberry

Blueberry

Sprincles three shades of coloured icing sugar in one twist

Twist half a turn and a beautiful flower will appear

No artificial food colours or flavourings

FOOD INSPIRES DESIGN

GRANDMA'S
RAISIN BREAD
INSPIRES
THE DESIGNER
TO CREATE
COMMUNITY
BAKERY

The Grandma

NAME
Mahmure

COUNTRY
Turkey

RECIPE
Raisin Bread

MAHMURE

Mahmure Yılmaz is 78 years old and originated from Giresun, a city in the Black Sea region in Turkey. She has lived in Istanbul since 1954. She used to cook raisin bread in an open-air hearth in the back garden. She placed a thick round stone, called a pileki on top of two bricks either side of the fire, and piled wood underneath. When the pileki stone became quite hot, she placed the bread on top of it and covered it with a metal plate. So that the bread and pastries inside would cook well, she placed wood embers from the fire on top of the plate. Her grandmother taught her how to bake raisin bread. She used to bake it for guests or on special occasions. Nowadays she bakes it especially for her daughters and her grandchildren because they love it.

RECIPE > HISTORY AND TRADITION

The origin of raisin bread is uncertain. This homemade bread is a recipe unique to the Yılmaz family. Both yellow grapes and wheat flour were rare ingredients in the Black Sea region. So this sweet pastry was only made in their family on special occasions. It was baked on a thick circular stone, called a pileki, which is well known in the Black Sea region. The pileki stone was especially used in the region for making corn bread and anchovy bread. Raisin bread may have originated from the culinary practices of Orthodox Christian communities of the Ottoman Empire. Noel bread, which was made with sultanas in the Orthodox Rum cuisine in Cappadocia, was similar to raisin bread.

The Recipe

RAISIN BREAD

INGREDIENTS

1.7kg bread flour
20g salt
30g sugar
15ml olive oil
400ml water
28g fresh yeast dissolved in 125ml of water
1kg sultanas (seedless yellow grapes)

PREPARATION

Combine the flour, salt, sugar, olive oil and water.
Add the fresh yeast and mix well.
Knead the dough for 10 minutes and add the sultanas
in the last minute. The dough should be slightly soft.
Place the dough in a lightly oiled tray large enough
for it to double in size.
Cover it with a cloth and leave it to rise for one hour.
Bake it in a preheated oven at 200°C for about
35-40 minutes.

The Designer

NAME & COUNTRY
Eva Závodná, Slovakia

EDUCATION
MSc in Architecture, Urbanism and Building
Sciences, TU Delft (NL)

FIELD OF EXPERTISE
Architectural design, food design
and food cultures

WEBSITE
http://evazavodna.wordpress.com
http://summertreats.wordpress.com

Based on your story I have designed a concept for "Community Bakery". An open place where people could learn about traditions of bread and also try to bake according to your recipe. There they could discover the joy of baking which you are a great example of.

It was a pleasure to learn from you!

Best wishes to you and your family!

Eva

The Concept

COMMUNITY BAKERY

CATEGORY

Interior Design For Food (IDFF)

DESCRIPTION

A community bakery can be located anywhere and it is open to everyone. It is a meeting place around good and genuine bread. The concept proposes a bakery pavilion where bread making is demystified and made available to the public. It houses a retail space and a small museum about bread, but mainly allows the visitors to prepare and bake their own loaves. For unskilled bakers this is a great opportunity to learn about bread, which they probably eat daily. For experienced bakers it can be a place to meet, share and enjoy baking. Mahmure's recipe and the traditional methods are preserved, but presented in a new and simple way. The negative aspects of baking at home (such as making a mess, the need to purchase a lot of ingredients and uncertainty about the recipe) are diminished. So now the greater public has access to genuine locally produced and almost home-baked "DIY bread".

How is bread made?
Daddy can we find
out? Lets make it!

Inspired by Saadet and Mahmure [Turkey]
Category Interior design for food
Author Eva Závodná

COMMUNITY BAKERY

Interior design concept which exposes the process of baking the most basic food item - Bread. Baking bread is demystified - anyone can learn about how it is made and prepare their own loaf.

INSPIRATION

The design was inspired by the stories of Turkish grandmothers Saadet and Mahmure, both preparing bread. They present baking as a social event when people from the neighbourhood would gather and bake together. Nowadays baking is done individually at home - the time devoted to baking is decreasing and so might be the skills. Community bakery creates a place where one can bake in company of others and with assistance of a skilled bakers. Preparations (like preparing the starter of yeast, mixing the dough, controlling the oven, cleaning and providing the dishes) are done for the visitor - which takes away the burden of cleaning and time spent on the baking. For less skilled bakers making bread is no longer a difficult task, which they would have to deal with alone. Children can visit and learn about making bread, which they probably eat every day. Skilled bakers can gather here and share their skills and knowledges. This new type of bakery is a meeting place around fresh and genuine food.

The design piece is a large scale product, which holds everything for preparing bread according to the traditional recipe. It can be placed inside a retail space or raised out on a public square or a park - resembling baking on an open air oven. Everything is placed on an elevated plane.

The visit starts at the main desk and an explanation board, which explains and describes the process of baking bread. Second part is where the visitors can see how the dough is made - the dough is prepared by skilled staff member and it is left to raise before it is given to the visitor. After getting their share of the dough and utensils, the visitor can choose the additional ingredients and work them into the dough on a nearby work tables.

The loaf shall be left to raise again, but only for a shorter amount of time. In this way the visitors can witness the process, but don't have to wait too long.

An important element of the bakery is a large oven. It is designed according to the open air stone ovens. After baking the bread should be cooled on the cooling rack and then it can be eaten or taken home by the visitor - now the new baker.

A small cafe and bread shop are part of the bakery.

The 'Community bakery' makes baking more understandable and reachable to the public. Unlike in the past everyone has an access to the oven but people lack time, confidence and practice in baking. By creating an environment where they can learn about the ingredients, process and tricks, people can familiarize themselves easily with the baking techniques. Exposing baking to the public can rise the interest over this activity.

The traditions are being kept, in details adapted to the 'faster' era. The element of socializing over a simple activity is as attractive today as it was in the past.

The question of origin of the food product that are being sold is becoming an important issue. Closer relation of the ingredients and the customer plays in favour of the current trends.

The pavilion is proposed primarily from wood, with a hidden steel structure. Some partitions are proposed to be from glass in order to achieve a sense of openness. The furnace oven is from stone, heat can be supplied by wood or by other means. The additional work tables and cafe seating is not included in the design, but it should be present around it. A gathering place with DIY Bread.

RECIPE

The bakery is focused only on bread. Departing from a simple recipe of the 'Village bread' by Saadet, Mahmure's 'Raisin bread' offers a new possibility for this treat. By adding other ingredients to the plain dough a large variety of flavoures can be created. Therefore only one type of dough is prepared in the bakery, but each visitor can add ingredients which transform the bread and make it unique. Then they truly create their own bread.

The ingredients and their amount to the dough remain as written in the Mahmure's recipe: 1700 g of bread flour, 30 g of sugar, starter - 28 g of yeast dissolved in 125 ml of water, 15 ml of olive oil, 400 ml water, 1000 g raisins, pinch of salt

However in order to allow variety, the raisins should be added after the dough has raised. The raisins can be replaced or combined with other ingredients - for example nuts, other dried fruits, seeds or even herbs and spices.

HOW DOES IT WORK

INNOVATING TRADITIONS

PLAN   SCALE 1:20

0   1m

0   5m

RESTING THE DOUGH
Bowl for first raising of the dough

DOUGH PREPARATION TABLE
Only for the staff

INGREDIENTS DISPLAY
Open shelf, covered with glass
Storage and display of the ingredients used for the dough preparation.

SECOND RESTING
Shelves for resting the dough on baking sheet before baking

ADDITIONAL INGREDIENTS
Free standing containers with the additional ingredients for flavouring the bread.

DESCRIPTION BOARDS, STORAGE
Storage of the additional ingredients, cupboard doors serve hold information

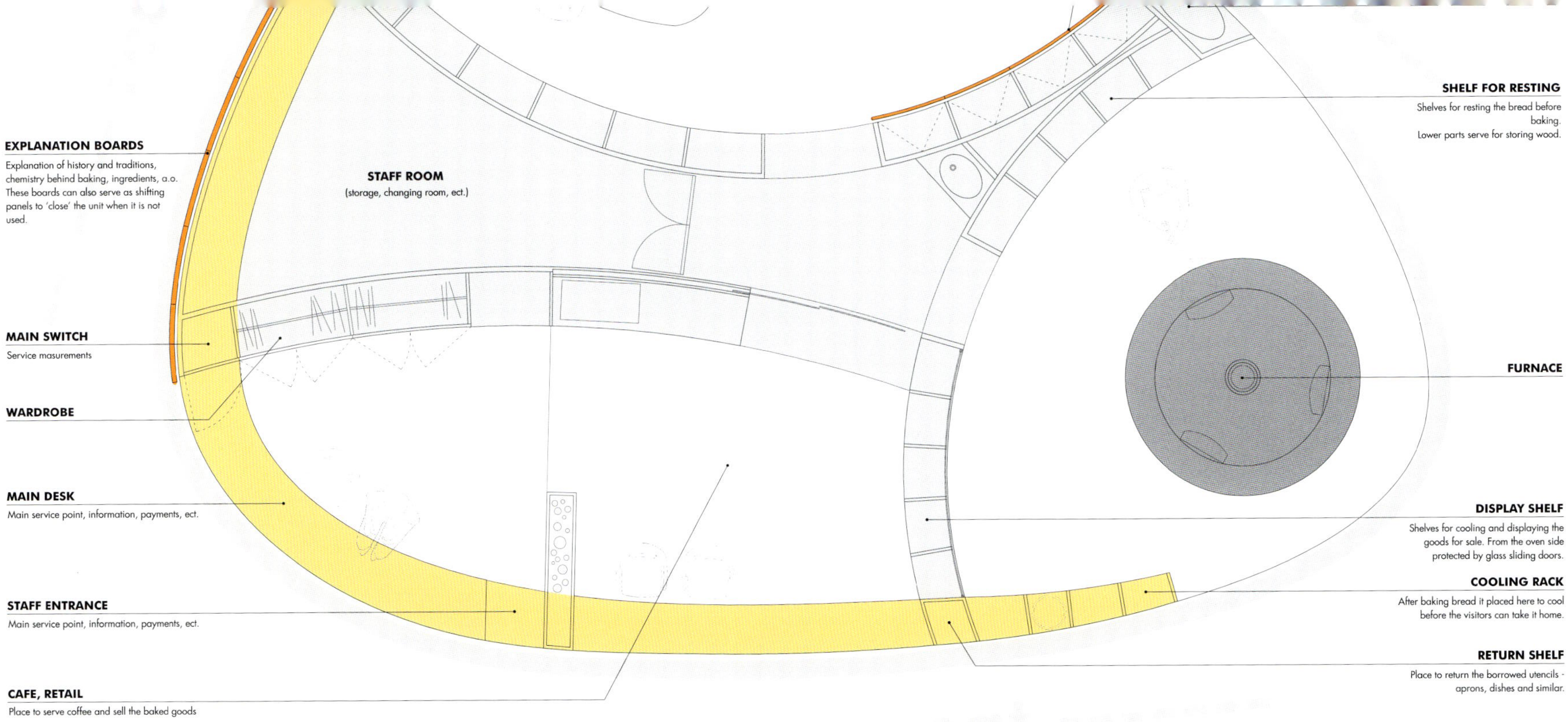

SHELF FOR RESTING

Shelves for resting the bread before baking.
Lower parts serve for storing wood.

FURNACE

DISPLAY SHELF

Shelves for cooling and displaying the goods for sale. From the oven side protected by glass sliding doors.

COOLING RACK

After baking bread it placed here to cool before the visitors can take it home.

RETURN SHELF

Place to return the borrowed utensils - aprons, dishes and similar.

STAFF ROOM

(storage, changing room, ect.)

EXPLANATION BOARDS

Explanation of history and traditions, chemistry behind baking, ingredients, a.o. These boards can also serve as shifting panels to close the unit when it is not used.

MAIN SWITCH

Service measurements

WARDROBE

MAIN DESK

Main service point, information, payments, ect.

STAFF ENTRANCE

Main service point, information, payments, ect.

CAFE, RETAIL

Place to serve coffee and sell the baked goods

VIEWS

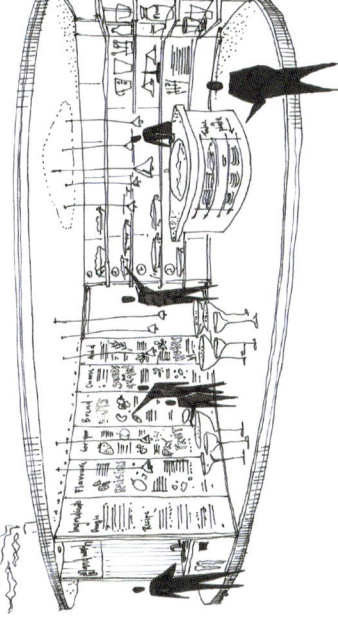

MAKING

View of space for choosing ingredients and preparation of dough

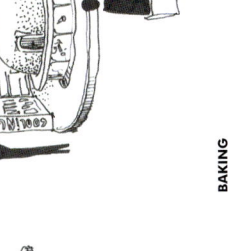

BAKING

View of preparation tables and oven space

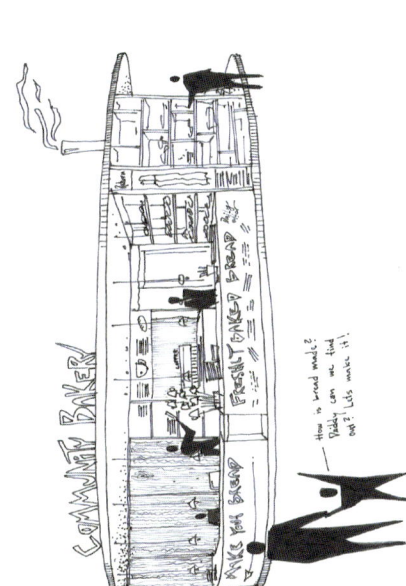

MAIN APPROACH

View of the main desk and retail space

FOOD
INSPIRES
DESIGN

GRANDMA'S
TWISTED BAKLAVA
WITH HAZELNUTS
INSPIRES
THE DESIGNER
TO CREATE
HOW TO MAKE
BAKLAVA

The Grandma

NAME
Emriye

COUNTRY
Turkey

RECIPE
Twisted Baklava with Hazelnuts

EMRIYE

Emriye Gül Abdik, is 78 years old, originated from Trabzon in the Black Sea region and has lived in Istanbul since 1958. She has been familiar with baklava since her childhood, when she learned how to make it from her mother and the older people in her family. Since the early days of her marriage, she has made it (both in the twisted shape and the classical one) for her family. Baklava is a dessert prepared for ritual events such as weddings, religious feasts and for receiving guests. Emriye still continues to make baklava for special occasions and makes it in the Black Sea region style, using hazelnuts for the filling instead of walnuts or pistachios. In the Black Sea region, baklava is usually filled with hazelnuts instead of walnuts or pistachios because they are one of the most important crops cultivated in the region. She also recommends using hot milk with sugar instead of syrup for soaking the baklava, as is done in Trabzon.

RECIPE > HISTORY AND TRADITION

Burma baklava, also known as coiled baklava (sarıgıburma), is an example of one of the many types of baklava that exist in Turkish cuisine. Ottoman cookbooks have included recipes for Burma baklava filled with walnuts since the 18th Century. The first reference dates back to the Anatolian Seljukide era in the 13th Century. During the Ottoman era, baklava became a refined dessert prepared in different styles in the Ottoman palace. It was also a popular dessert among the people of Anatolia as well as other parts of the empire, such as the Balkans and the Arabian Peninsula. Many references to baklava can be found both in Ottoman archival records and in popular literature. The most important technical detail in the preparation of baklava is to make very thin sheets of pastry called yufka with a special rolling pin called an oklava. The origin of yufka dates back to the 11th Century nomadic Turkish culinary culture of Central Asia. Food historians conclude that baklava is a synthesis of both nomadic Turkish and medieval Arab cuisines. In Anatolia, baklava resulted from the nomadic technique of making yufka and the Arabian desserts soaked in syrup.

TWISTED BAKLAVA WITH HAZELNUTS

INGREDIENTS

For the dough:
750g wheat flour
1/2 tsp salt
300ml water

For rolling:
300g wheat starch

For the filling:
500g hazelnuts

For brushing the dough:
375g butter

For the syrup:
1kg granulated sugar
600ml water
1 tsp lemon juice

PREPARATION

The dough:
Sift the flour and salt onto a work surface and make a large hollow in the centre. Pour 150ml water in the middle and mix in a circular motion, drawing in flour from the outside. When sticky, add the remaining water and continue to mix until a soft dough is formed. If necessary, add some flour. Knead well until very smooth and elastic. Then allow to rest for 15 minutes under a clean cloth. Roll the dough out to a 30cm log shape and cut it into 15 evenly sized pieces (each 60g). Shape each piece into a ball. Then allow to rest for another 15 minutes.

Rolling out:
Generously dust the working surface with starch and roll out each piece of dough to 20cm using a rolling pin. Dust the dough with starch while rolling it out until almost transparent and 30-40 cm in diameter. Meanwhile preheat the oven to 200°C.

The filling:
Sprinkle chopped hazelnuts over the sheet of pastry and then roll it up with a thin rolling pin (1cm diameter). Crinkle the pastry roll by pushing toward the middle from each end. Push it off the rolling pin and place it on a tray. After you have prepared all the pieces of dough in the same manner, place them on a tray and cut each rolled pastry into three parts.

Brushing and baking:
Pour melted butter over the pastry.
Bake until brown on top and golden on the bottom.
Leave to cool on a wire rack.

The syrup:
Make syrup by gently dissolving the sugar in water. Pour the hot syrup over the burma baklava and allow to soak for several hours, turning occasionally.

The Designer

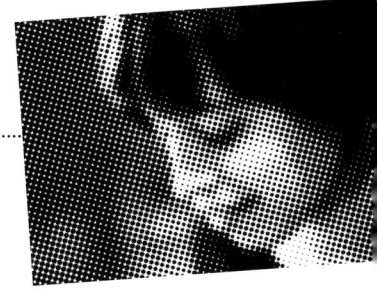

NAME & COUNTRY
Manolya Isik,
the Netherlands

EDUCATION
Photography at the Willem de Kooning
Academy in Rotterdam

FIELD OF EXPERTISE
Photography

WEBSITE
http://www.howtomakebaklava.com

Emriye Gül Abdik, dear grandma!

Thank you for letting me use your beautiful recipe. I made a website, inspired by your baklava, where you can scroll through the recipe step by step, and I used some funny characters to also make it attractive to children. I hope more people will (try to) make baklava after they scroll through the story.
Thanks again & iyi günler!

– Manolya Işık.

The Concept

HOW TO MAKE BAKLAVA

CATEGORY

Design About Food (DAF)

DESCRIPTION

My concept is an online interactive guide to making baklava. It shows children the beautiful process of making baklava, step-by-step. Besides photography, there are two other things I have always loved: Illustration and food. Now I combine them all together. I would be glad if my work could encourage people of all ages to become more interested in food, and I want to share my views in a beautiful and useful way.

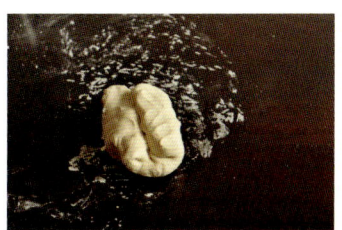

all right.
let's slice the
DOUGH
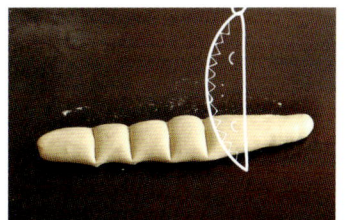

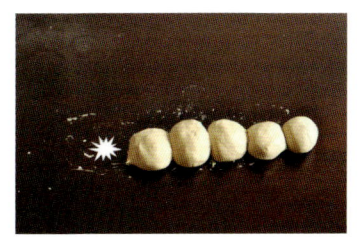

hammer
time

remember to
keep an eye
on it

HOW TO MAKE baklava

An interactive guide to making baklava.

Showing children the beautiful process of making baklava, step by step.

Inspiration:
Twisted Baklava with Hazelnuts

I heard this lovely Turkish grandma say that she learned

making baklava when she was young, by looking at her

older family members. Her (grand)children now, however,

are too busy with school to learn how to make baklava the

both Turkish, I was born in the Netherlands) and so I was wondering how I could show the making of this traditional dish to children, in a fun and accessible way. I remember what kind of special experience it was to watch my grandma making baklava: the fact that you could make an elastic ball by mixing only flour and water and kneading patiently for 15 minutes, and the way my grandma rolled out the dough to sheets so thin you could look straight trough them. First we baked the baklava until it was golden and crunchy, and then we poured hot syrup over it so it became deliciously sticky and juicy.

I want children to know how much fun it is and how beautiful the process of baking is, so I decided to create a visual story about making baklava. You follow every step of the process by navigating trough the story yourself, and at the end you can print the recipe and start making your own baklava for real!

The project is already online, you can check it out here:

www.howtomakebaklava.com

hammer time

remember to
keep an eye
on it

FOOD INSPIRES DESIGN

GRANDMA'S
QUICK-READY
CAKE
INSPIRES
THE DESIGNER
TO CREATE
QUICK-READY
CAKE ROOF

The Grandma

NAME
Annie & Martha

COUNTRY
Belgium

RECIPE
Quick-Ready Cake

ANNIE & MARTHA

Martha and Annie are two sisters who have been living together in their parents' house for over sixty years. They both love cooking, but Annie is the baking specialist. Annie's mother wanted one of her children to continue baking forever. Annie thought it should be her. She's still baking now, after more than fifty years. She makes her own bread, her own French pistolets and, of course, her own cakes. She only visits a bakery to see how the baker works.

RECIPE > HISTORY AND TRADITION

The 'quick-ready-cake' is made with the leftovers of other dough. These leftovers are reused to make new dough. The batter doesn't take much work either. That's why the cake is called 'a-quick-ready-cake'. According to both sisters, this was the only cake that could be eaten hot. All the other cakes had to cool down for a couple of hours. When the quick-ready cake was baked, they put it on the roof. It was ready to eat while it was still lukewarm.

The Recipe

QUICK-READY CAKE

INGREDIENTS

a cake mould
125ml liquid (milk and water)
300g flour
a pinch of salt
20g yeast
1 tsp sugar
60g butter
1 large egg
1 egg yolk

For the batter:
2 apples
cinnamon
8 tsp sugar
125g butter

PREPARATION

Heat the water and the milk until the mixture is lukewarm. Pour the flour into a bowl. Make a hollow in the
middle. Sprinkle the salt around the edge of the hollow.
Crumble the yeast into the middle of the hollow. Pour
the lukewarm liquid on the yeast. Add a tablespoon of
sugar. Mix with some extra flour. Let the dough rise for
15 minutes. Add the butter and the egg. Knead well
until smooth and elastic. Let the dough rise for half an
hour. Mould it into a ball and let it rise again for half an
hour in a bowl covered with a damp towel. When it has
risen, roll it out. Place the dough in a preheated cake
mould. Prick the dough with a fork. Let the dough rise
for another 15 minutes. Rub the crust with egg yolk.
The batter: Peel the apples and slice them. Cover the
dough with the apple slices. Sprinkle some cinnamon
on the apples. Then mix the butter with the sugar and
top the apples with this mixture. Finish with some
knobs of butter. Place the cake in a preheated oven for
20-25 minutes at 200°C. Remove and serve lukewarm.

The Designer

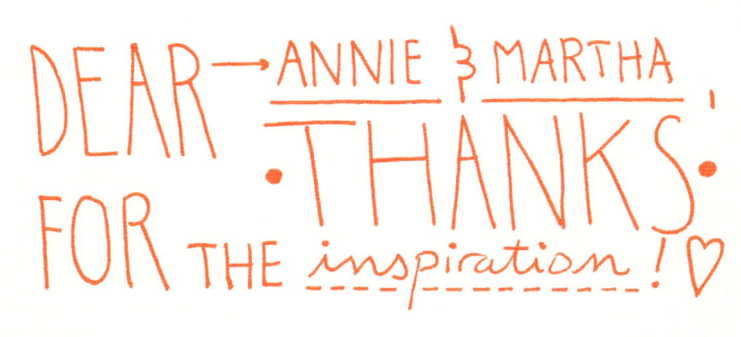

NAME & COUNTRY
Hannah Vranko, Croatia

EDUCATION
BA studies in Product Design
(School of Design, Faculty of Architecture,
University of Zagreb, CRO)

FIELD OF EXPERTISE
Food design

CONTACT
hannah.vranko@gmail.com

DEAR → ANNIE & MARTHA
THANKS
FOR THE inspiration! ♡

The Concept

QUICK-READY CAKE ROOF

CATEGORY

Design For Food (DFF)

DESCRIPTION

The terracotta 'quick-ready cake roof' is an object designed to present, serve and tell a story about a Belgian dessert by sisters Annie and Martha. It mainly functions as a cake heat indicator and a cooler enabling the cake to be served and consumed at the perfect temperature, and of course, quickly!

My concept is based on a quote spotted in the recipe's video: "When the cake was taken out of the oven, we placed it on a roof to cool. It was really hot, so it had to cool." The object is multifunctional as it also serves as a bowl for storing apples, which are one of the main ingredients of the quick-ready cake!

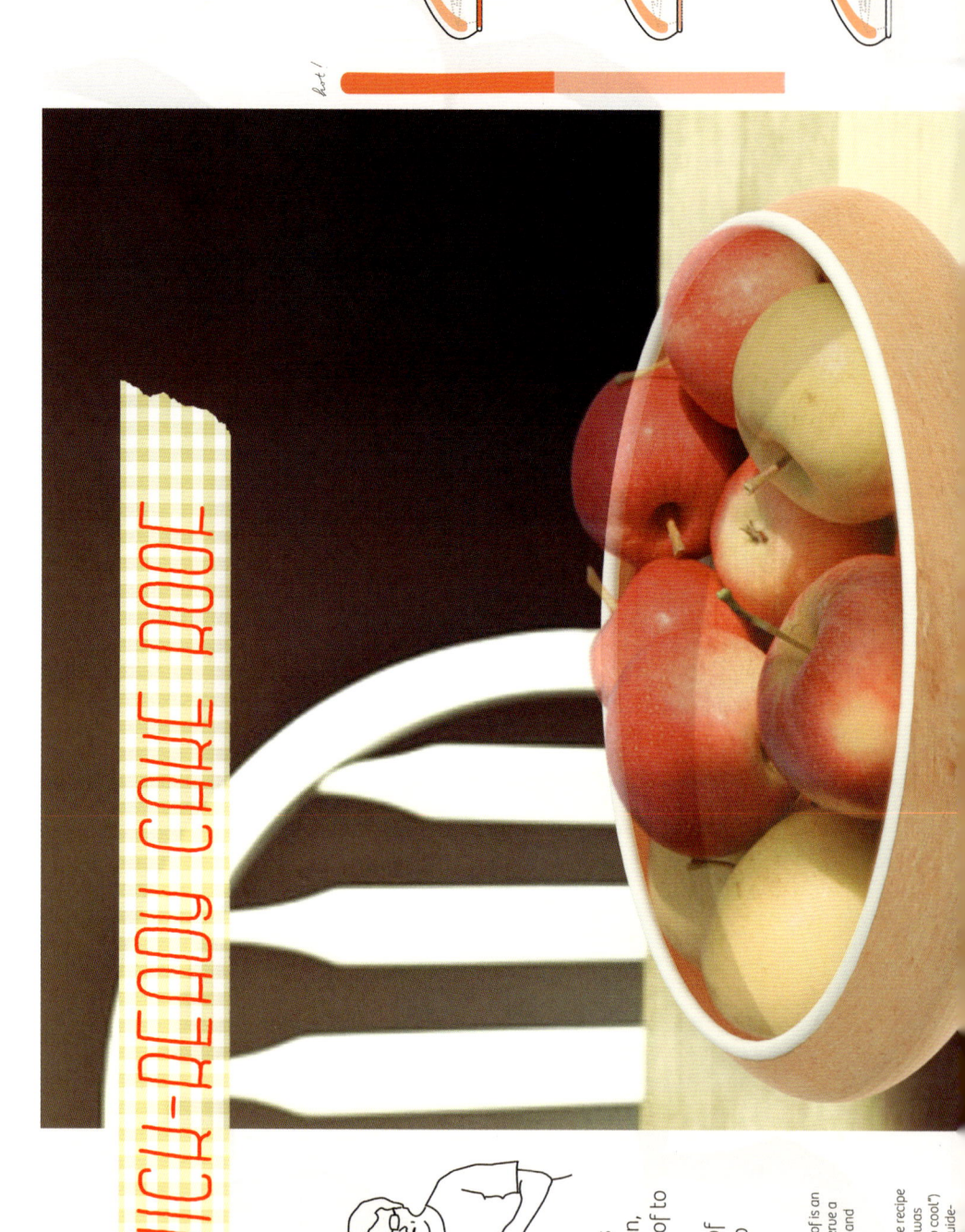

QUICK-READY CAKE ROOF

"When the cake was taken out of the oven, we placed it on a roof to cool. It's really hot when it comes out of the oven, so it has to cool."

Terracotta Quick-Ready Cake Roof is an object designed to present and serve a particular Belgian dessert. Annie and Martha's "Quick-Ready Cake".

Finding the very first line from the recipe video intriguing ("When the cake was ready, we placed it on the roof to cool") it inevitably became a concept guide-

Another resemblance is a choice of material—belgian terracotta clay, which, when raw, acts like dough and takes its final form when baked. Besides, its colour directly recalls the most common type of roof tiles!

In addition to terracotta clay, there is a top and bottom temperature sensitive non-skid lining that serves as the Quick-Ready Cake's heat indicator. At a room temperature, it is calm white while when exposed to a low, e.g. fridge temperature, it changes to warming red and it is ready to use as a cake roof!

A steaming hot, straight-from-the-oven cake is being covered with a cold terracotta lid which slowly cools the cake. Porosity of the material disables the condensation inside of the Quick-Ready Cake Roof and the opening on top serves as a real chimney. Once the red lining has turned white, the Quick-Ready Cake is ready to eat!

Quick-Ready Cake Roof' dimensions are slightly variable due to the making process, which is by hand on a classic pottery wheel. The shape is asymmetrical and seems to visually change with different use.
Finally, when the small opening is facing down, a bowl for storing the most important Quick-Ready Cake ingredient appears!

perfect!

meaning. Thinking about preserving the tradition (serving the cake when lukewarm) but slightly changing the action (avoiding actually placing it on the roof) all without abandoning the roof context, a small scale roof-inspired object was designed.
Character of the object was intended to resemble the character of the cake; beautifully imperfect, unique and preserving a crafty, human touch.

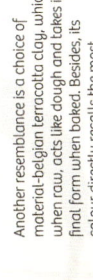

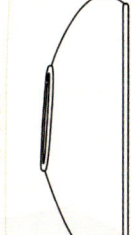

Hannah Vranko for

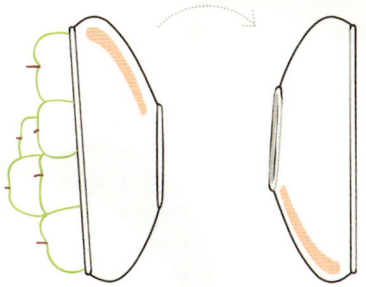

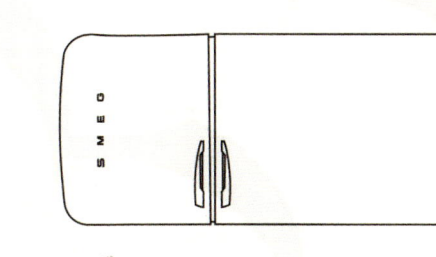

SMEG

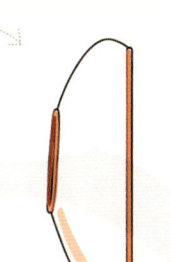

FOOD INSPIRES DESIGN

GRANDMA'S
KATMER
INSPIRES
THE DESIGNER
TO CREATE
MAMA

The Grandma

NAME
Fatma

COUNTRY
Turkey

RECIPE
Katmer

FATMA

Fatma Samancı, is 67 years old and originates from Konya, a city in Central Anatolia. In Konya, pastries are very much in demand and are made quite often. Like katmer, layered pastries, pies and varieties of baklava have remained in Fatma's mind since childhood. Konya is the wheat region, so flour was abundant in every household, in gunnysacks. Katmer is a pastry dessert mostly baked in the rural areas. Before going into the fields, peasants baked katmer and other pastries because they were easy to make and eat. Fatma remembers how her aunt used to bake it in her village. Since the homes never used to have ovens, katmer was baked on a metal plate or copper pan. She learnt how to make pastries from her father. She also used to bake bread with him in an oven built by him. He was the first one to let her roll filo pastry. Katmer is often baked at home during the month of Ramadan. Bakeries also make it before breaking the fast and sell it. In the past, it was just an ordinary dish and was not really sought after, but nowadays it is attracting attention in Istanbul as a different flavour, especially if it is made with tahini.

RECIPE > HISTORY AND TRADITION

Katmer is an ancient pastry. The earliest written reference dates back to the end of the 14th Century during the Ottoman era, though it may be even older. According to some historians, katmer has been present in Central Asian Turkish cuisine since the 11th Century. In 17th Century Istanbul, it was among the pastries sold in bakeries. Katmer is known in most Turkish regions and it can be consumed as a savoury or sweet pastry. It is made in the same way as flat bread (yufka) and baklava, but unlike yufka, the katmer dough has a generous amount of butter and oil. Katmer can be prepared plain or stuffed with tahini, poppy seed paste or walnuts. In Gaziantep, a city in the southeast region, it is made with ground pistachios; in Afyon and Usak they make it with poppy seed paste. Katmer filled with tahini (a paste made from ground sesame seeds) is renowned, especially in Konya. It can be eaten plain and also as a sweet pastry, served with jams, grape molasses or icing sugar. Katmer has always been baked on a metal plate or copper pan, but nowadays it is also baked in the oven.

The Recipe

KATMER

INGREDIENTS

For the dough:
360g all-purpose flour
10g salt
200ml water
1 egg
80ml olive oil
200g tahini
250g melted butter

For the coating:
icing sugar

PREPARATION

Combine the salt with the sifted flour. Make a hollow in the centre and add water, egg and olive oil.
Mix well until the dough is soft. Knead until smooth.
Divide the pastry into 12 pieces and roll each piece into a tight ball. Arrange on a floured surface and leave to rest for 15 minutes under a slightly damp towel.
Place a piece of pastry on the lightly floured work surface and roll it out into a circle (30cm diameter). The pastry must be very very thin. Spread some butter and tahini over the circle of dough and roll it up tightly. You may sprinkle a little sugar as well. Then form it into a circle in a spiral shape. Press out then roll it again gently and place it on a greased oven tray. Repeat these steps for all the pieces of dough. Bake the katmer in a preheated oven at 200°C for 20 minutes.
Dust with icing sugar or serve hot with jam or honey.

The Designer

NAME & COUNTRY
Cyril Leroux, Eléonore Samier
and Romain Vince, France

EDUCATION
All students at L'École de Design Nantes Atlantique,
New Eating Habits option; Eléonore: BTS in
the Design of Communication Space and Volume

FIELD OF EXPERTISE
We are from different, but complementary
backgrounds

WEBSITE
http://eleosamier.com
http://cargocollective.com/romainvince

Dear Fatma,

We would like to say thank you. Your recipe inspired our project.
After having watched the video, where you prepare your
Katmer, several times, we were sure to work for your cake.
We like the way you cook and your natural gestures. We really
want to try to present your cake on our plate ! The final scene
of the video only confirms that this cake tastes better if you
share it with your family or your friends ! We wish you all the
best and many more good recipes.

Eleonore, Cyril and Romain

The Concept

MAMA

CATEGORY

DFF

DESCRIPTION

We watched all videos before choosing the one we would like to work on. We were interested in Turkish cuisine, especially the Katmer made by Fatma. We chose her video because of the way this grandma shares her expertise and for her cooking gestures. Being a widow, uniting her family is really important to her. She loves sharing cakes with her family, which is why we decided to work on a concept related to the sense of sharing. After watching the video, we noticed that the grandma bakes the cake intuitively, because the recipe is part of her past. We are especially interested in the transition between taking the cake out of the oven and eating it. From our point of view, everything happens at this moment. The beautiful presentation makes us want to eat. Flowers are omnipresent in Fatma's video: on her apron, her flower-shaped cake... This pattern was an inspiration: the dish is the heart of the flower and the plates are like petals. Our brand is called Mama because of the association of Fatma's name and the name of her cake, the katmer (mère being the French word for mother). Mama is also a Turkish nickname for a mother or a grandmother.

mama

By Cyril Leroux//Éléonore Samier//Romain Vince

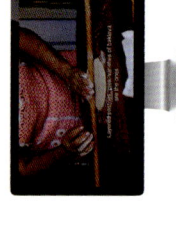

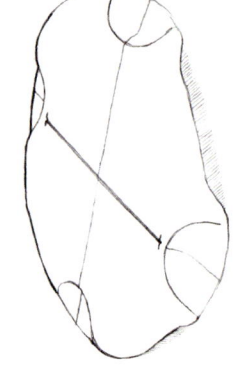

We watched each video before choosing the one we would like to work on. We were interested in Turkish cuisine especially Fatma & Katmer. The way this grandma shares her expertise and cooking gestures made us choose her video. She is a widow and unifying her family is really important to her. She loves sharing cakes with her family, that is why we decided to work on a concept related to the sense of sharing.

After watching the video, we noticed that cooking the cake is intuitive because its recipe is part of this grandma's history.
We are especially interested in the transition between taking the cake out of the oven and eating it. From our point of view, everything happen at this time. A beautiful presentation makes us want to eat.

Flowers are very present in Fatma's video : on her apron, her flowered shaped cake... This pattern was an inspiration, the dish is the heart of the flower and the plates are like petals.
Our brand is called Mama because of the association of Fatma's name and the name of her cake, the Katmer.

Our project is to work on tableware.

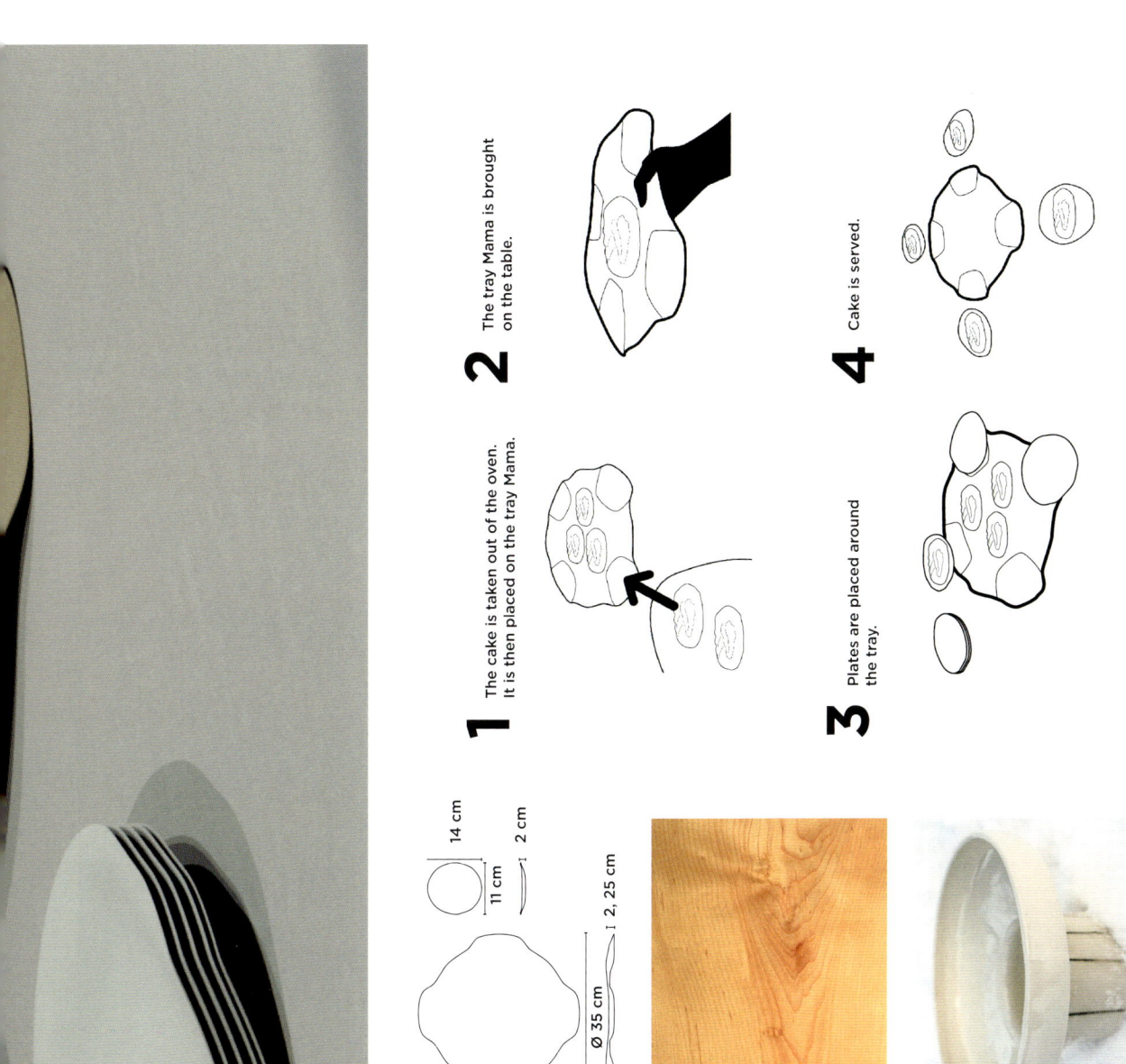

1 The cake is taken out of the oven. It is then placed on the tray Mama.

2 The tray Mama is brought on the table.

3 Plates are placed around the tray.

4 Cake is served.

14 cm

11 cm

2 cm

Ø 35 cm

Ø 35 cm

2, 25 cm

First of all, we choose the maple wood because it is strong enough to resist to the cake cuting. We used ceramic for plates because it is able to keep the heat ant it has a very smooth texture. It also allowds us to apply it on a color patern.

FOOD INSPIRES DESIGN

GRANDMA'S
RICOTTA & WILD
CHERRY TART
INSPIRES
THE DESIGNER
TO CREATE
RICOTTA & WILD
CHERRY TART

The Grandma

NAME
Oretta

COUNTRY
Italy

RECIPE
Ricotta & wild cherry tart

RECIPE > HISTORY AND TRADITION

Ricotta and wild cherry tart is a baked dessert made from a short crust base typical of the Lazio confectionary tradition. Particularly sought after by the inhabitants of Rome, these kinds of jam tarts were apparently greatly appreciated by pope Pio IX, who often enjoyed this dessert after his meal. The principal ingredients of this seasonal dessert are closely linked with the pastoral tradition of the region, and include sheep's milk ricotta (typical of sheep farming in Lazio) and wild cherries *(Prunus cerasus visciola)*, an acidic fruit that is not too sweet and particularly suitable for tarts and preserves.

The Recipe

RICOTTA AND WILD CHERRY TART

INGREDIENTS

a baking tin

For the short crust pastry:

300g flour

150g sugar

3 egg yolks

150g butter

a pinch of salt

the white of one egg

For the filling:

400g sheep's milk ricotta

200g wild cherries (or 250g of redcurrant jam)

140g sugar

2 eggs

the rind of one lemon, grated (use untreated lemons)

50g icing sugar

PREPARATION

The day before:

Place the ricotta to drain in a colander, as it must be perfectly dry and free from whey (it is best to leave it overnight in the refrigerator). Remove the stones from the wild cherries and place them in a bowl.

The short crust pastry:

Use only chilled ingredients. Mix the sieved flour and the sugar and make a hollow in the mixture. Add the egg yolks, the cold butter cut into cubes and a pinch of salt.

Work it all together quickly. To make the dough softer and to help it bind better, add an egg white.

When the dough has come together, roll it into a ball, wrap it in cling film and leave it to rest in the refrigerator for at least a couple of hours.

Grease a baking tin well and sprinkle it with flour.

Roll out the pastry to a thickness of 1cm and place it in the tin. Remove any pastry that hangs over the edges, cut it into strips and put it aside.

The cream filling:

Heat the oven to 170°C.

Combine the ricotta, sugar and eggs in a bowl.

Add the grated lemon rind and stir well to obtain a creamy mixture. When the mixture is ready, spread it evenly over the short crust base in the baking tin.

Then arrange the well-drained wild cherries on top. (Alternatively, spread an even layer of wild cherry jam over the creamy mixture).

Use the strips of remaining short crust pastry to make a crosshatch design on the top of the tart.

Bake the tart in the middle of a preheated oven at 170°C for about 40 minutes. Cover it with aluminium foil if it browns too quickly. When it is ready the top of the tart should be lightly browned.

Allow the tart to cool in its tin, then place it on a serving dish, dust with icing sugar and serve in thin slices.

The Designer

NAME & COUNTRY

Antonella Mignacca, Italy

EDUCATION

Course at the Polytechnic
of Milan in Food Experience Design

FIELD OF EXPERTISE

Food design, my motto being: "Design with
the stomach, Eating with Love!"

WEBSITE

www.intothefood.eu

The Concept

RICOTTA AND WILD CHERRY TART

CATEGORY

Food Product Design (FPD)

DESCRIPTION

Jam tarts in general are very popular in Italy, with or without the ricotta. If you make small portions you will have a more customizable product for trying out different flavours at the same time. The pastry may change colour depending on the jam filling and the texture may also vary. The tarts can be filled with different jams, providing a greater range of taste sensations.

SALT

SUGAR

EGG YOLKS

EGG WHITE

BUTTER
CUT INTO CUBES

LEMON
GRATED

FLOUR
SIEVED

RICOTTA and WILD CHERRY TART

1 - MAKE THE SHORTCRUST PASTRY

SALT

SUGAR

EGG YOLKS

EGG WHITE

BUTTER
CUT INTO CUBES

LEMON
GRATED

FLOUR
SIEVED

LEMON
GRATED

INGR...
FOR
FLOU...
3 EGG...
THE
BUTT...
SUGA...
THE
UNTR...
SALT

2 - WORK IT TOGETHER AND MAKE IT INTO A BALL

CLINGFILM

REFRIGERATOR

2 HOURS OF REPOSE

3 - PREPARE AND BAKE THE SMALL TART ⏱ 30 MIN - 150°

ROLL OUT
THE PASTRY

GREASE THE SMALL STEEL
CYLINDRES FROM PASTRY

CUP A SIDE
OF CYLINDER

CUT INTO A STRIP
THE PASTRY
AND WRAP THE CYLINDRES

WITH SMALL
PORTION
YOU CAN
HAVE A MORE
COSTUMIZABLE
PRODUCT

YOU CAN TR...
DIFFERENT
FLAVORS AT
THE SAME
MOMENT

4 - FILL THE SMAL...

PASTRY

EGG

GRATED

FOR THE FILLING
WILD CHERRIES 200 G
OR 250 G OF REDCURRANT JAM
SHEEP'S MILK RICOTTA 400 G
SUGAR 140 G
ICING SUGAR 50 G
GRATED LEMON

RICOTTA

ICING SUGAR

JAM

YOU CAN USE
FILL THEM
WITH
DIFFERENT
JAM HAVING
MORE CHOISE

THE PASTRY
CAN CHANGE
COLOR OR
TEXTURE DEPEN
DING ON THE
JAM FILLING

TASTE!

MADE IN ITALY

HISTORY
RICOTTA AND REDCURRANT TART
IS A BAKED DESSERT WITH A
SHORTCRUST BASE TYPICAL OF
THE CONFECTIONARY TRADITION
OF LAZIO,PARTICULARLY SOUGHT
AFTER BY THE INHABITANTS OF
ROME, THEY SEEM TO HAVE BEEN
VERY MUCH APPRECIATED BY
POPE PIO IX, WHO OFTEN ENJOYED
THIS DESSERT AFTER HIS MEALS.

PIO IX

THE PRINCIPAL INGREDIENTS OF THIS
SEASONAL DESSERT ARE CLOSELY
LINKED WITH THE PASTORAL
TRADITION OF THE REGION

FOOD
INSPIRES
DESIGN

GRANDMA'S
JAN IN A BAG
INSPIRES
THE DESIGNER
TO CREATE
JAN IN A BAG

The Grandma

NAME
Gaby

COUNTRY
Belgium

RECIPE
Jan in a Bag

GABY

Gaby was one of seven children from a farming family. Every Saturday she had to go to school while her mother cleaned the house. Because mum didn't have a lot of time to make lunch, she always made Jan in a bag. Jan in a bag was the perfect meal for Saturday, the cleaning day.

RECIPE > HISTORY AND TRADITION

This recipe is popular in Meetjesland, a region not far from Bruges and Ghent where Gaby grew up.
Many cookery books confirm its existence, only the origin is uncertain. One book says it's a Dutch recipe, while another says it comes from East Flanders.
Jan in a bag is even mentioned in a diary of an Australian soldier in World War I who ate it during the war. The best way to eat it is to serve it with a milk sauce, with butter, and if you like, with vanilla and dark sugar.

JAN IN A BAG

INGREDIENTS

1 egg
1 cup of milk
300g flour
25g yeast
a handful of dried grapes,
briefly soaked in water

For the sauce:
1/4l milk
100g butter
brown sugar
optional: a fresh vanilla pod

PREPARATION

Beat the egg with half the milk in a bowl. Add the flour.
Dissolve the yeast in the rest of the lukewarm milk.
Add this to the mixture. Add the grapes and knead
well until elastic.
Take a clean towel and place it in a bowl. Sprinkle some
flour on the towel. Put the dough on the towel in the
bowl. Place the bowl in a warm place where the dough
can rise. Leave it there for at least two hours.
Take a large pot filled with water. Bring to the boil.
When the water is boiling, add the towel with the
dough. Make sure the towel is tightly wrapped around
the dough. Leave it for 3/4 hr.
Remove it from the water and remove the dough from
the towel. Place it on a serving plate.

The sauce: Melt the butter in the heated milk.
You can add a fresh vanilla pod.
Slice the dough and pour the hot milk on the slices.
Sprinkle a lot of brown sugar on top and serve.

The Designer

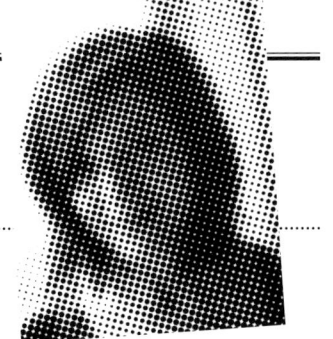

NAME & COUNTRY
Léa Bougeault
and Jessica Pigeron (Miit Studio), France

EDUCATION
Graduates from the Design School in Lyon

FIELD OF EXPERTISE
Food experience design for companies
and creative consultancy for the industry,
Miit studio

WEBSITE
www.miit-studio.com

Dear Gaby,

Here in France, we are used to eating
bread every meals. But it was the
first time I heard about cooking the bread
dough in a towel.
Your recipe, simple and authentic as I
like, intrigued me.
That's why I chose it to design a new
food product. I made some changes
but I hope you will recognize your
original "Jag in a bag".

Kind regards,

Léa

The Concept

JAN IN A BAG

CATEGORY

Food Product Design (FPD)

DESCRIPTION

Our project is inspired by a traditional Belgian recipe for simmering a ball of bread dough in a towel for three hours. This cooking method gives a soft melting texture to the bread, which is served with a vanilla sauce and brown sugar. We wanted to adapt the recipe for mass production, while preserving the essential elements of the traditional Belgian recipe, achieving the authentic flavour and texture, with the original ingredients and a convenient cooking method. Our Jan in a bag consists of little frozen bread bites filled with vanilla sauce. Agar-agar is added to the sauce to make a ball-shaped jelly sauce. The bread dough is then wrapped around the jelly balls, so that the sauce melts inside as the bread bite cooks. The cooked bread bites are then rolled in brown sugar. The result is a warm, sweet and crispy snack that melts in your mouth. Jan in a bag is a good compromise for people who don't have the time to bake. It's very simple and easy to make. The fabric packaging is cooked directly in boiling water for about 30 minutes. This packaging allows the bread to be cooked, but it's also eco-friendly. The fabric is produced without the use of harsh chemicals and pesticides and is biodegradable.

Roll the bread bites in brown sugar.

A warm, sweet and crispy snack that melts in your mouth.

JAN IN A BAG / Miit Studio

> Jan in a bag are sweet treats made with ball-shaped jelly sauce covered with bread dough.

(The packaging is made with organic linen fabric.)

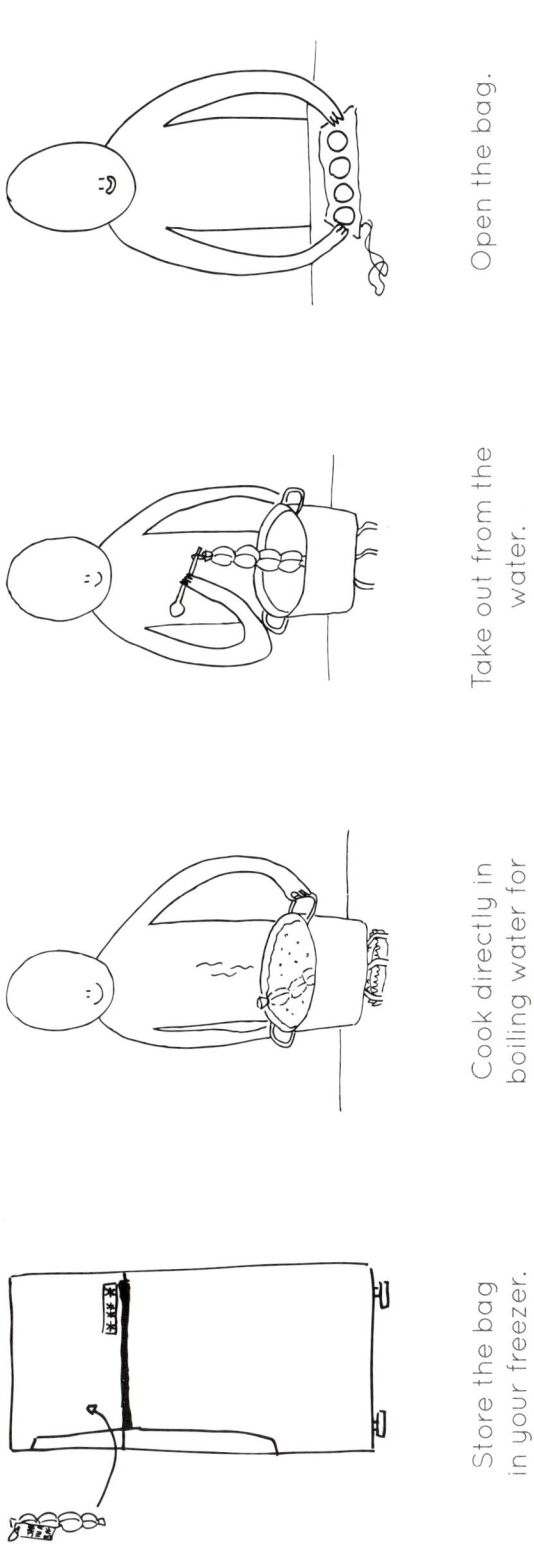

Open the bag.

Take out from the water.

Cook directly in boiling water for about 30 minutes.

Store the bag in your freezer.

A warm, sweet and crispy snack that melts in your mouth.

Roll the bread bites in brown sugar.

Vanilla sauce + Agar-agar

Raisin

Bread dough

Jan in a bag / Léa Bougeault and Jessica Pigeron / Grandma's design competition

FOOD INSPIRES DESIGN

GRANDMA'S
BILBERRY
RYE PIE
INSPIRES
THE DESIGNER
TO CREATE
BILBERRY RYE
PIE CAKES

The Grandma

NAME
Milja

COUNTRY
Finland

RECIPE
Bilberry Rye Pie

Bilberry rye pie or mustikkakukko belongs to the culinary tradition of the South and North Savo regions of Eastern Finland. In the region, rye flour is used traditionally and baked with a filling inside the crust (the kukko pastry). A savoury version of the dish, kalakukko, is widely known and was granted TSG (Traditional Speciality Guaranteed) status in 2002. Sweet mustikkakukko is based on ingredients once gathered from local fields and forests. Wheat flour is now also used in the dish, but the Finnish still pick bilberries during the season, from July to September. This traditional delicacy has now spread throughout Finland. To make it, the dish is lined with dough, and the bilberry filling is added and covered with the top crust. Mustikkakukko is usually served warm with whipped cream, vanilla sauce or ice cream, as a dessert or with coffee.

BILBERRY RYE PIE

INGREDIENTS

For the pastry:
150g butter (room temperature)
50ml sugar
300ml rye flour
1/2 tsp baking soda

For the filling:
1-1 $^{1/2}$l bilberries (depending on the size of the pie dish)
1 tbsp potato flour
100-150ml jam sugar/sugar

PREPARATION

Heat the oven to 180°C.

The pastry: Combine the soft butter with the sugar. Mix the baking soda into the rye flour. Add the flour-soda mixture into the butter-sugar mixture and whisk well together in an ovenproof china bowl. Set aside about 1/3 of the pastry for the lid of the pie. Use the rest (about 2/3) of the pastry to line the china bowl.

The filling: Mix the ingredients and spoon into the china bowl lined with the pastry. The bowl must be filled right up to the top as the berries sink a little.

Roll the remaining pastry into a lid, at least the size of the bowl, and place it on top of the blueberries. Use a chopping board to transport the lid without breaking it. Bake for 1-1 $^{1/2}$ hours in the preheated oven. Let the pie cool a while, and serve with vanilla ice cream or vanilla sauce. In winter, instead of fresh bilberries, use frozen.

The Designer

NAME & COUNTRY
Raija Niemi, Finland

EDUCATION
Master's degree in Education

FIELD OF EXPERTISE
Home Economics teacher for 36 years,
now retired

WEBSITE
http://keittion.blogspot.fi

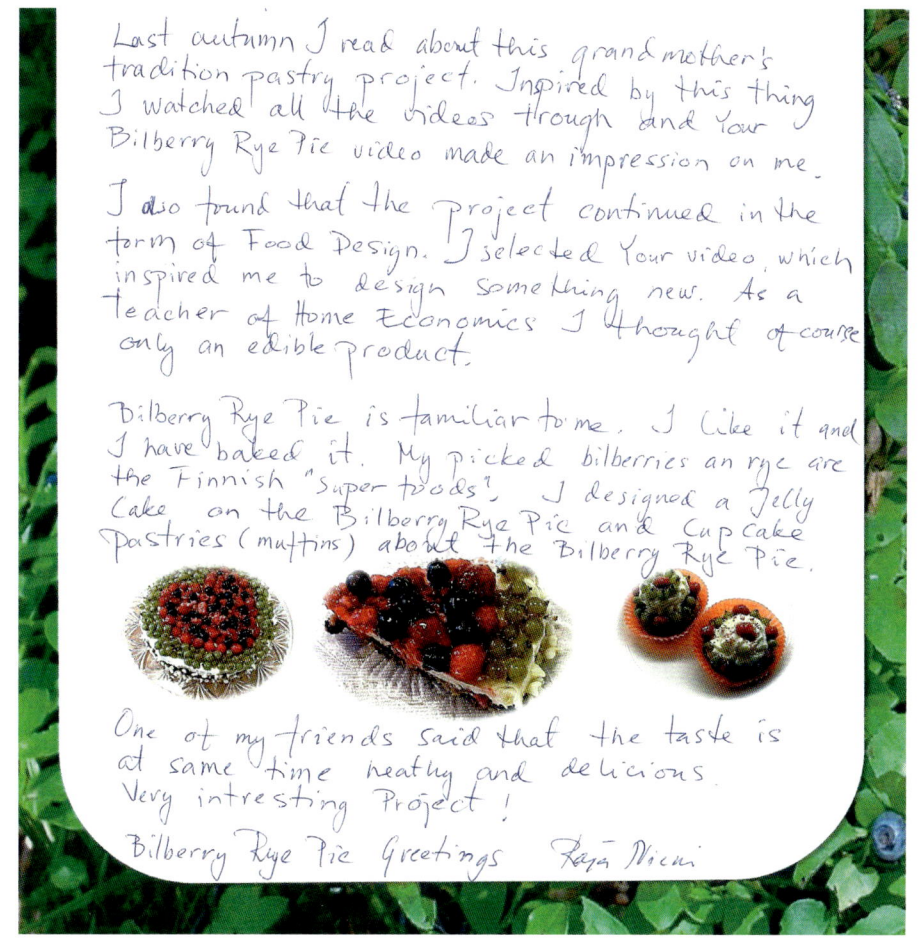

Last autumn I read about this grandmother's tradition pastry project. Inspired by this thing I watched all the videos trough and Your Bilberry Rye Pie video made an impression on me.

I also found that the project continued in the form of Food Design. I selected Your video, which inspired me to design something new. As a teacher of Home Economics I thought of course only an edible product.

Bilberry Rye Pie is familiar to me. I like it and I have baked it. My picked bilberries an rye are the Finnish "super foods". I designed a Jelly Cake on the Bilberry Rye Pie and Cup cake Pastries (muffins) about the Bilberry Rye Pie.

One of my friends said that the taste is at same time heathy and delicious. Very intresting Project!

Bilberry Rye Pie Greetings   Raija Niemi

The Concept

BILBERRY RYE PIE CAKES

CATEGORY

Food Product Design (FPD)

DESCRIPTION

My design product is inspired by the bilberry rye pie mustikkakukko by Grandma Milja Komi from Finland. I also live in the region, where mustikkakukko is a traditional pastry, although I had not heard about this kind of cake with a thin mustikkakukko base before... I have made the pie and I like it very much. One of my friends even said that this is a "health pastry", but it tastes very good anyway.

I have designed a modern pastry using the traditional bilberry rye pie, which I believe could be baked commercially as well. In my version, I used different berries for decoration.

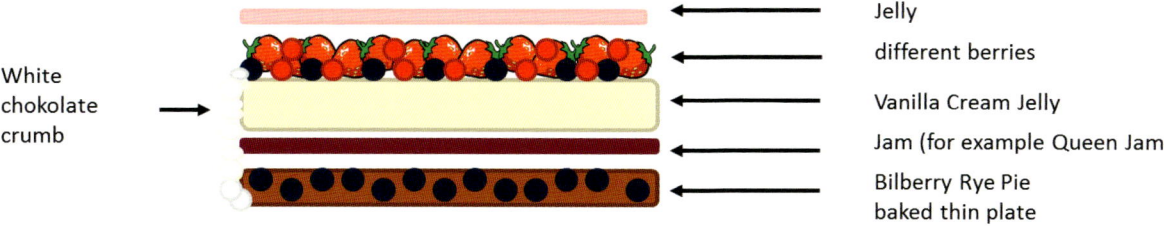

White chokolate crumb

Jelly

different berries

Vanilla Cream Jelly

Jam (for example Queen Jam)

Bilberry Rye Pie baked thin plate

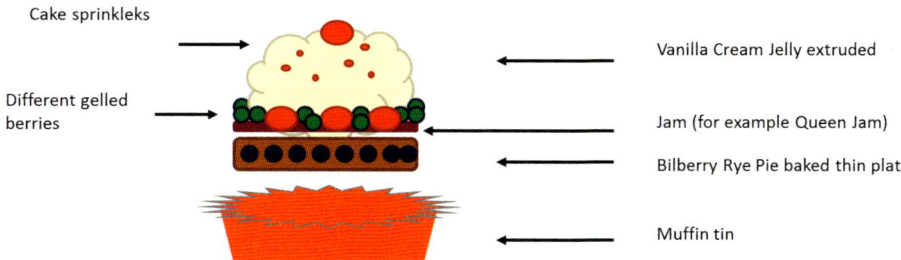

Cake sprinkleks

Different gelled berries

Vanilla Cream Jelly extruded

Jam (for example Queen Jam)

Bilberry Rye Pie baked thin plate

Muffin tin

Bilberry Rye Pie Cakes

I have chosen my design product the Bilberry Rye Pie "Mustikkakukko" by Grandma Milja from Finland. I have made the pie and I like it very much. I live also in the region, where "Mustikkakukko" is a tradition pastry.

This pastry contains Finnish raw materials. The bilberry and the rye belongs to healthy food stuffs . I also used different berries for decoration. One my friend said, that this is a health pastry, but however it tastes very good.

My category is Food Product Design. I have designed a modern pastry using the traditional bilberry rye pie. I have not before tasted the cake, which bottom is a thin "mustikkakukko" or heard about this kind cake. I think, that by this way the Bilberry Rye Pie can to make in bakeries

Bilberry Rye Jelly Cake

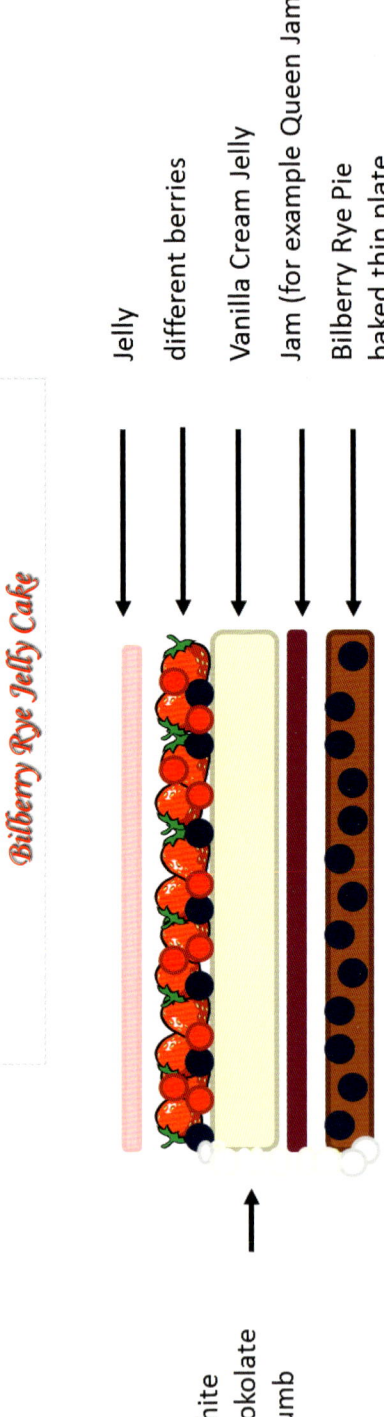

White chokolate crumb

Jelly

different berries

Vanilla Cream Jelly

Jam (for example Queen Jam)

Bilberry Rye Pie baked thin plate

Bilberry Rye Cupcake

Vanilla Cream Jelly extruded

Jam (for example Queen Jam)

Bilberry Rye Pie baked thin plate

Muffin tin

Cake sprinkleks

Different gelled berries

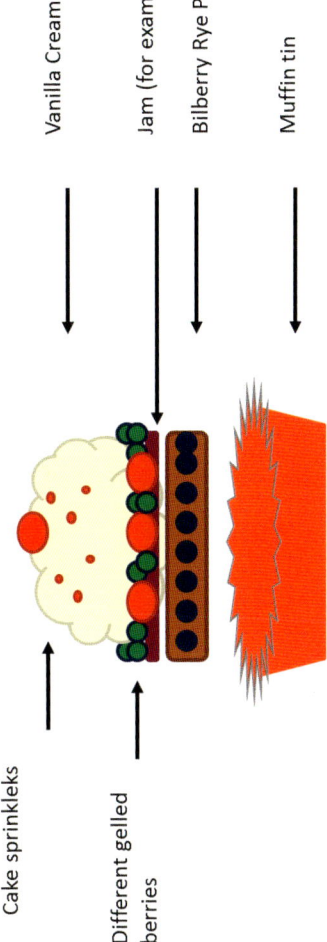

FOOD
INSPIRES
DESIGN

GRANDMA'S
GALUCIU
INSPIRES
THE DESIGNER
TO CREATE
LIKE GRANDMA

The Grandma

NAME
Giovannina

COUNTRY
Italy

RECIPE
Galuciu

RECIPE > HISTORY AND TRADITION
Grandmother Giovannina's cakes are reminiscent of those from her childhood, when she worked in the family bakery. The cakes were baked in all different shapes, but the most common were the cockerel and the round one.

GALUCIU

INGREDIENTS

700g of dough already risen
100g butter
flour
50g oil
50g sugar,
300g raisins
a pinch of salt

PREPARATION

The day before
Start by preparing the yeast eight hours prior
to processing. Solve the yeast in lukewarm water, add
the flour (1 kg), mix, knead and cover the dough to rise.

The next day
Melt the butter and combine with the batter.
Add the oil. Then start to knead vigorously and add
flour until the dough is elastic and saturated.
Divide the dough in 2 equal parts, stretch and roll
them with the rolling pin, giving each part the shape
of a rooster.
Cover 1 'rooster' layer with raisins. Then top it with
the other layer of dough. Create the shape of the legs,
the comb and stick a raisin where the eye comes.
Rub the rooster with water and sprinkle the sugar
on top. Bake at 170°C for 45 minutes.

The Designer

NAME
Alice Conquand,
Caroline Fourier,
Alexandre Leduc

COUNTRY
France

EDUCATION
Graphic design students at l'École de Design
Nantes Atlantique, in France. We are following
the same master course called "New Eating
Habits", which explores environmental and
health issues from an ethical viewpoint

FIELDS OF EXPERTISE
Alice is more at ease with building strong
design concepts, so her skills have been
essential in this part of the project.
On the other side, Caroline and Alexandre
brought sensibility and technical skills
to the illustration aspect, allowing us to
materialise what we had in mind.

WEBSITE
http://www.behance.net/aliceconquand
http://cargocollective.com/Alexandreleduc
http://www.behance.net/carolinefourier

Dear Giovannina,

I would like to thank you for the inspiration you gave us through
our Galaciu's recipe.

The first time we saw your video, we enjoyed the relationship you hav
with your granddaughter. Our design concept is based on the
relationship between parents or grandparents and their children o
grandchildren. This relationship is important because it permits
to transmit a know-how. Here, it is about cooking.
... to facilitate this transmition between two generations.

The Concept

LIKE GRANDMA

CATEGORY

Design About Food (DAF)

DESCRIPTION

Our concept "Like Grandma" is a playful, intuitive and educational application for iPad. In grandma Giovannina's recipe, the notion of transmitting one's know-how seems essential. Giovannina, a former Italian baker, is introducing her grand-daughter to cooking while making a Galuciu.. Here, the grandmother assumes the role of a teacher. Her kindness, glasses and dark round eyes illustrate her wisdom and traditional know-how, which we associated with the symbol of the 'owl'. The way she sprinkles the sugar on the cooked dough, the raisins that surprisingly appear inside the cake, the transformation of the dough into an animal-shaped cake and the minimal use of tools conjure up a magical scene. The little girl who is too young to cook by herself tries to copy her grandmother's gestures as best she can. The dough becomes a sort of game, a playful way for the little girl to cook like the adults, in spite of the kitchen being a sacred place reserved for grown ups only. With our app, children are introduced to cooking. They can follow traditional recipes guided by the owl as they play the game. Just like a lesson, the child uses the app first to learn how and then makes the recipe for real at the end. The whole atmosphere, the colours, the shapes, the furniture and the tools used in the app are based on our analysis of the video.

Like Grandma

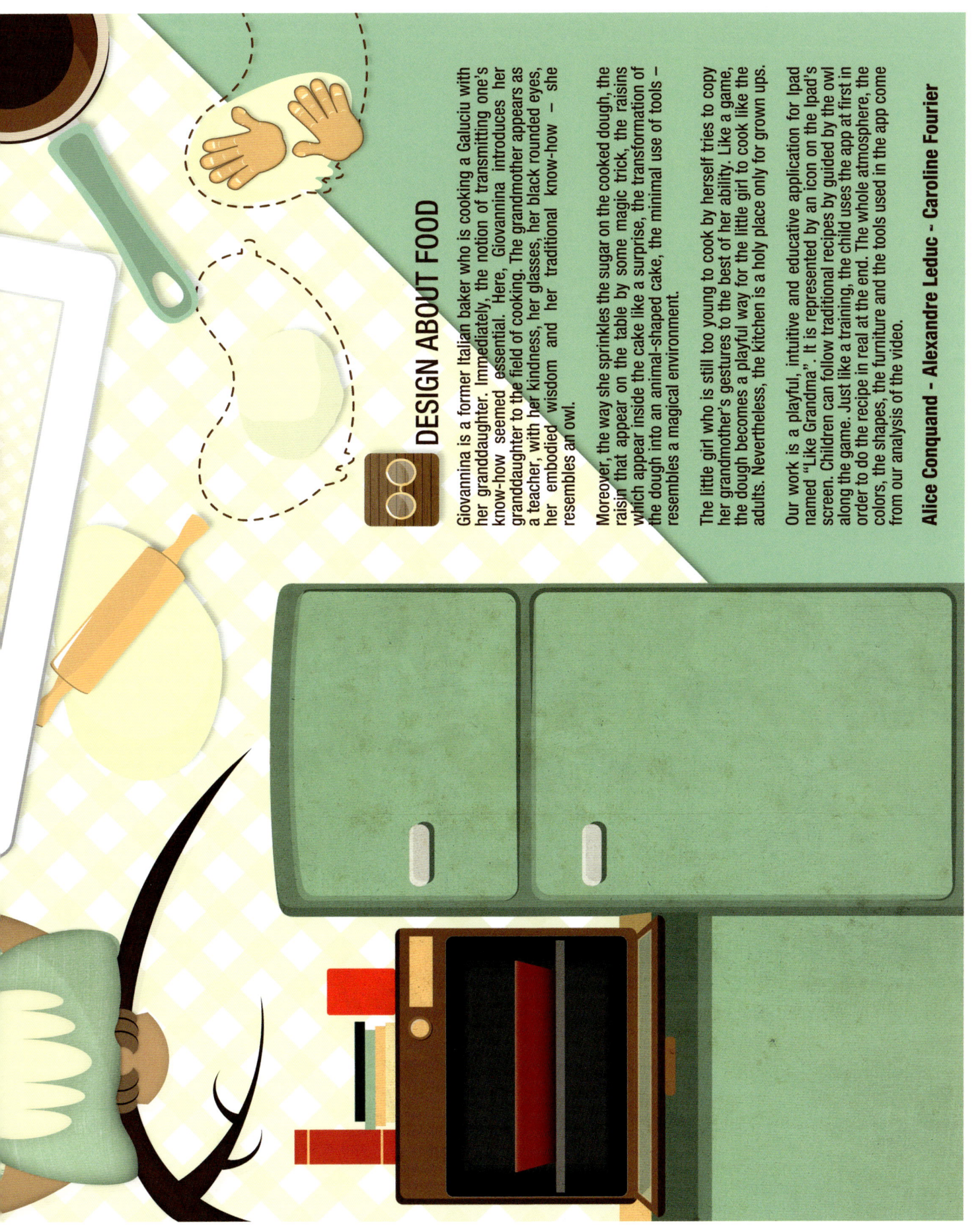

DESIGN ABOUT FOOD

Giovannina is a former Italian baker who is cooking a Galuciu with her granddaughter. Immediately, the notion of transmitting one's know-how seemed essential. Here, Giovannina introduces her granddaughter to the field of cooking. The grandmother appears as a teacher, with her kindness, her glasses, her black rounded eyes, her embodied wisdom and her traditional know-how – she resembles an owl.

Moreover, the way she sprinkles the sugar on the cooked dough, the raisin that appear on the table by some magic trick, the raisins which appear inside the cake like a surprise, the transformation of the dough into an animal-shaped cake, the minimal use of tools – resembles a magical environment.

The little girl who is still too young to cook by herself tries to copy her grandmother's gestures to the best of her ability. Like a game, the dough becomes a playful way for the little girl to cook like the adults. Nevertheless, the kitchen is a holy place only for grown ups.

Our work is a playful, intuitive and educative application for Ipad named "Like Grandma". It is represented by an icon on the Ipad's screen. Children can follow traditional recipes by guided by the owl along the game. Just like a training, the child uses the app at first in order to do the recipe in real at the end. The whole atmosphere, the colors, the shapes, the furniture and the tools used in the app come from our analysis of the video.

Alice Conquand – Alexandre Leduc – Caroline Fourier

FOOD INSPIRES DESIGN

GRANDMA'S
PEPERNOTEN
INSPIRE
THE DESIGNER
TO CREATE
PEPERPACK-
PACKAGING
CONCEPT FOR
PEPERNOTEN

The Grandma

NAME
Annie

COUNTRY
the Netherlands

RECIPE
Pepernoten

ANNIE

Grandma Annie always ate pepernoten during the early December Sinterklaas holiday. She remembers that when she was a child, she used to crawl through the house searching for pepernoten on the floor. Eating pepernoten is a very old tradition in the Netherlands.

RECIPE > HISTORY AND TRADITION

Pepernoten are usually eaten during the early December Sinterklaas (Saint Nicholas) holiday in the Netherlands. Sinterklaas is a typical Dutch tradition, though it is celebrated in other parts of Europe as well. In the Netherlands, Sinterklaas' Eve (5th December) is the main occasion for gift giving. A particularly distinctive custom associated with pepernoten is throwing handfuls of them throughout the room so that children can look for them. It was originally an ancient fertility ritual (like a farmer sowing seeds).

PEPERNOTEN

INGREDIENTS

2 baking sheets
20g wheat flour
1/2 tsp baking powder
1/2 tbsp aniseed (chopped)
1/2 tbsp cinnamon
1/2 tbsp nutmeg (ground)
1/2 tbsp cloves (ground)
1/2 tbsp ginger (ground)
a pinch of salt
160g brown sugar syrup

PREPARATION

Preheat the (hot air) oven to 160°C.
Sieve the flour into a bowl. Mix the baking powder,
aniseed, cinnamon, nutmeg, cloves, ginger and salt
through the flour. Make a hollow in the flour and pour
in the syrup. Stir the syrup from the outside inwards
into the flour. Knead the dough until it becomes a ball.
Grease two baking sheets.
Form about 20 marble-sized balls. Place them on the
2 sheets, so that they are the same distance from each
other. Flatten each ball slightly. Bake for 20 minutes
in the oven or until golden brown.

The Designer

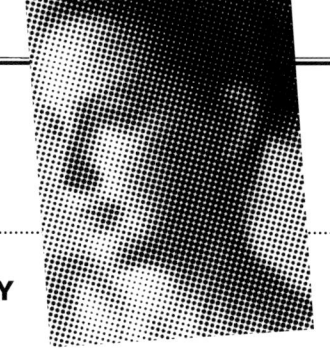

Thank you Annie!

I didn't know what to expect when I entered the Grandma Design competition. When I saw your recipe, I got inspired and worked with inthusiasm.

The playfulness of the cookies, and the wonderful story behind them gave me an idea of a fun packaging for them. I tried to bring the pastry available for everyone in an environmentally friendly, inspiring and delightful way. The colorful packages include your recipe, so anyone can try them at home.

I have to say I really enjoyed working with this project, and hopefully giving a chance for baking tradition to live on.

Hope you'll have a wonderful autumn, thank you again!

Kiitos from Finland

- Satu Lustig

NAME & COUNTRY
Satu Lustig, Finland

EDUCATION
Tammerkoski art high school and bachelor's degree from the Lahti Institute of Design and Fine Arts majoring in jewellery design

FIELD OF EXPERTISE
After graduating I have worked as a freelancer designing jewellery, websites and illustrations and setting up my first exhibitions

WEBSITE
www.behance.net/satulustig

The Concept

PEPERPACK- PACKAGING CONCEPT FOR PEPER- NOTEN

CATEGORY

Design For Food (DFF)

DESCRIPTION

This packaging concept pays tribute to the pepernoten tradition. It functions as a means of transportation, presentation, preservation and communication for the baked product. The shape of the box and the illustration support the playful nature of the round biscuits and show the tradition of throwing the cookies around the house for delighted children to find. However the colour scheme is suitable for other occasions as well, not just the Sinterklaas holiday in December.

With this packaging I aimed at bringing the fun tradition of throwing the pepernoten to a larger audience. The original recipe is found on the pack, enabling everyone to bake them for themselves. On the bottom, people can find information about the Food Design Competition and the baking traditions in the different countries.

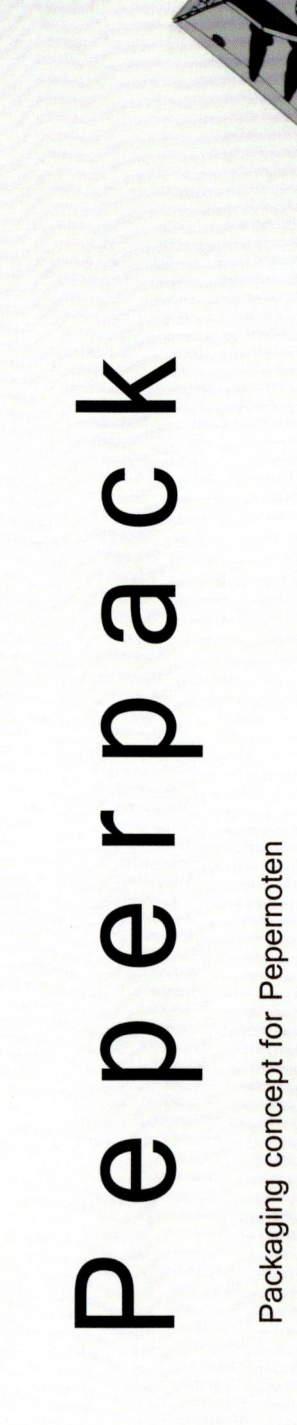

Peperpack

Packaging concept for Pepernoten
Satu Lustig, Finland
Inspired by grandma Annie, Netherlands

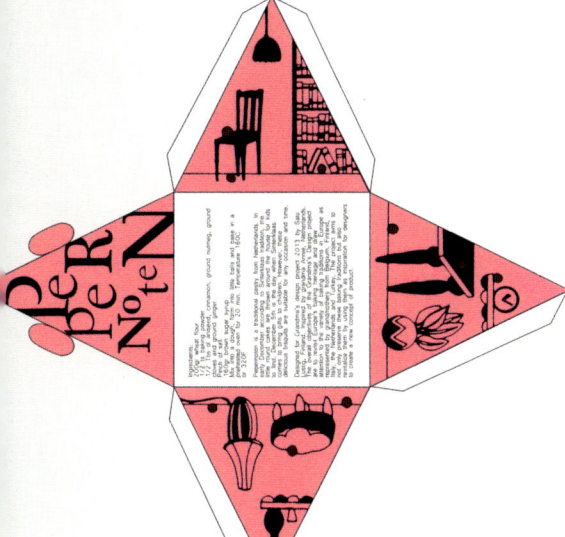

My
inspiration was
grandma Annie from Netherlands.
The playfulllness of the traditional pastry
made me think of fresh ways to bring it out
to the public. The main startingpoint was the
communication of the product. I wanted it to suit
many occasions, not only as its traditional role in the
Sinterklaas tradition.

Grandma Annie

The functionality of the pastry itself was hard to
miss, and the packaging I designed enhances the
playfullness of the delicious little cake. I thought
that the pastry should not be a delight of one
season, but suitable whenever there is
a time to enjoy something small
and sweet.

The
illustration on the boxes
is inspired by the playful tradition
of the Pepernoten. The Sinterklaas' Eve
(December 5th) is when kids recieve their gifts.
"Black Peter" distributes the Pepernoten for kids
before the arrival of Sinterklaas himself. The biscuits are
thrown in a room by the handfuls for the delighted children.
In the illustration you can find the little biscuits scattered in a
room, hidden for you to find.

Illustration and tradition

The idea is, that the box is an elegant gift or a place to store
the Pepernoten. I wanted the pastry to have a new and also
more elegant role. The different colors in packaging and
the graphics enable the product to be used in catering
of various occasions: dinners, barbecues,
summer parties, bruch etc.

The
boxes are made of
food industry proofed cardboard.
The material withstands the grease
produced by the pastry. The boxes are easy
and ecological to transport unassembled to the
bakers.

Ecological

The assembled boxes interlock and are space-
efficient to transport. The idea is, that you can also
use the boxes over and over again with your
own bakings. When the boxes are worn out,
it is safe to recycle them with energy
waste or by paper-recycling.

Information about the
competition can be found at the
base of the package. It introduces the
aim to revive the baking tradition of chosen
competition countries, thus adding awareness
in the cause of this design copetition. Also the
original recipe is printed on the package.

Communication

As well as being a delightful container, my design
works as a messenger passing on information
and tradition. The illustration and written
information are designed to introduce the
delightful Sinterklaas tradition to a
wider public.

FOOD
INSPIRES
DESIGN

GRANDMA'S
HAPPINESS CAKE
INSPIRES
THE DESIGNER
TO CREATE
CLOCKWORK
CAKE

The Grandma

NAME
Beppa

COUNTRY
Italy

RECIPE
Happiness Cake

RECIPE > HISTORY AND TRADITION
The happiness cake was invented by Beppa's grandfather, Angel, who made many cakes for his daughters and family friends. Eating desserts together was a good opportunity to spend time together with friends and family. Beppa remembers her grandfather as a very kind man who always dedicated a lot of time to her when she visited him. The recipe itself is very simple and contains all local ingredients, typical of country life.

HAPPINESS CAKE

INGREDIENTS

a baking tin
50g currants
500g pumpkin, peeled and cleaned
2 apples
4 eggs
400g sugar
4 tbsp olive oil
500g flour
rind of 1 lemon, grated
100g corn flour
1 tbsp rum
1 packet of yeast
icing sugar to decorate

PREPARATION

Leave the currants to soak for half an hour in a bowl
of warm water.
Cook the pumpkin in the oven. When it is ready leave it
to cool and then mash with a potato masher.
Cook the apples and mash them with a fork, forming
a cream.
Break the eggs into a bowl and beat them with a whisk,
adding the sugar, then the oil. Incorporate the flour
little by little. When the flour is completely absorbed,
add the other ingredients and mix everything well.
Grease the baking tin, pour the mixture into it and cook
in a preheated oven at 180°C for about 40 minutes.
Once the cake has cooled, turn it out onto a serving
dish, dust with icing sugar and serve.

The Designer

NAME & COUNTRY
Florin Alexa-Morcov,
Romania

EDUCATION
Ph.D. Student in Design (National University of Arts, Bucharest), Master in Social Anthropology and Community Development (Faculty of Sociology and Social Work, Bucharest University), Degree in Design (Faculty of Decorative Arts and Design, Design Department, National University of Arts, Bucharest)

FIELD OF EXPERTISE
Food design, traditional food and food packaging design

WEBSITE
www.atelier-d.ro

Dear Beppa Grandma,

In the video presentation of your cake you spoke very touching about your family, about heritage and your grandparents. Your family story (including grandpa Angel) inspired me to create a physical cake recipe (an object not just a piece of paper), an object that could remain part of the family heritage for the next generations. It's a clockwork recipe mechanism with a time counter in order to mark the main operations. I want to thank you for the inspiration and I wish you and your family many happy years to come.
I share the love, affection and respect for your heritage!

Best regards,
Designer Florin Alexa-Morcov

The Concept

CLOCKWORK CAKE

CATEGORY

Food Product Design (FPD)

DESCRIPTION

The Clockwork Cake is a visual timing system that has been designed to simplify the recipe invented by Grandpa Angel for a new generation of users. We live in an era of timing, we usually calculate every operation that we intend to do in a day. Grandma Beppa however is not very explicit about the timing of all the food operations of her recipe. The clockwork cake recipe could be a solution: it is rather a coordinator of the main operations than an exact timing machine.

The principle is very simple. All the main baking operations are split up into visual fragments (including the ingredients), representing the timing. The clockwork starts working by turning the key. Each time an operation should be finished, you are informed by a mechanical sound system. This system is powered by a clockwork mechanism using a key.

The Clockwork Cake is environment friendly: it does not need any batteries and can be easily repaired if necessary.

As an object, the clockwork cake recipe could be an important souvenir for tourists visiting Grandma Beppa's specific area. Not to forget that the recipe was invented by Grandpa Angel, Beppa's grandfather, so it is already part of the family heritage, and by extension of that Italian region of Veneto. When tourists discover food specific to a region, they usually ask for the recipe. The Clockwork Cake allows them to physically take this recipe with them. This way, the physical recipe can become a powerful image in a kitchen which can be transmitted over generations.

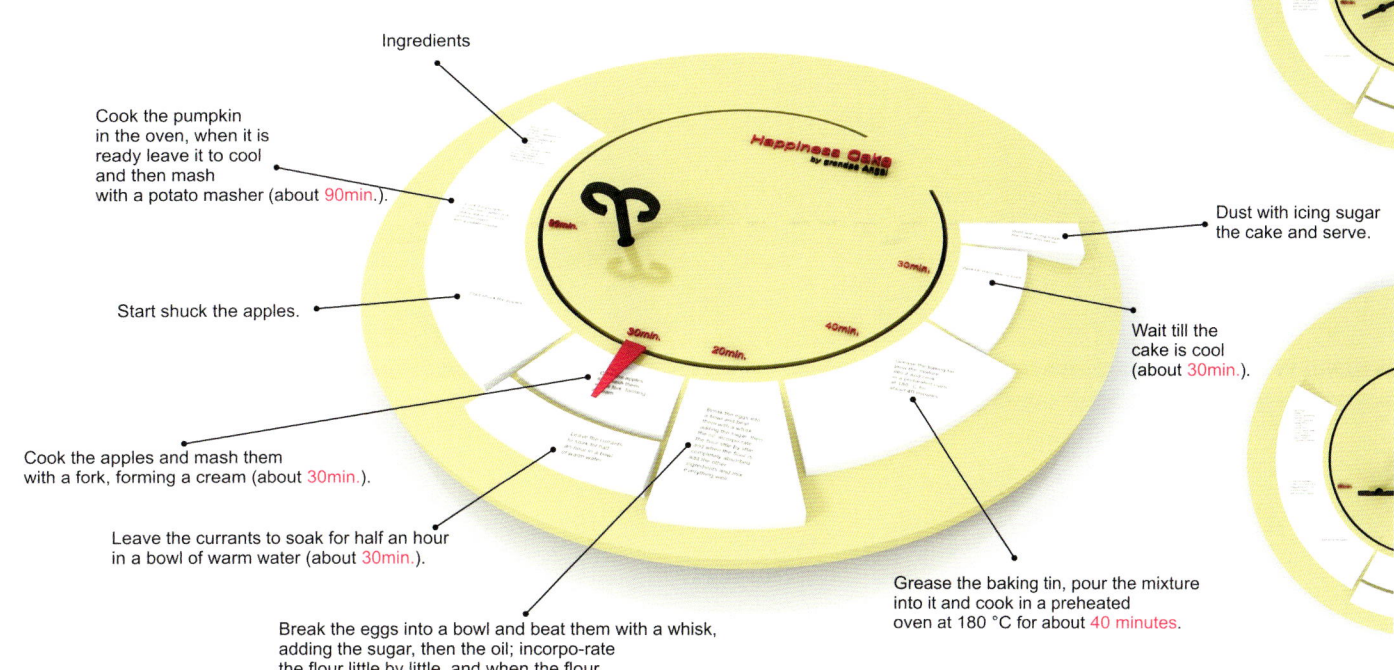

Ingredients

Cook the pumpkin
in the oven, when it is
ready leave it to cool
and then mash
with a potato masher (about 90min.).

Dust with icing sugar
the cake and serve.

Start shuck the apples.

Wait till the
cake is cool
(about 30min.).

Cook the apples and mash them
with a fork, forming a cream (about 30min.).

Leave the currants to soak for half an hour
in a bowl of warm water (about 30min.).

Grease the baking tin, pour the mixture
into it and cook in a preheated
oven at 180 °C for about 40 minutes.

Break the eggs into a bowl and beat them with a whisk,
adding the sugar, then the oil; incorpo-rate
the flour little by little, and when the flour
is completely absorbed, add the other ingredients
and mix everything well (about 20min.).

Happiness Cake
by grandma Beppa

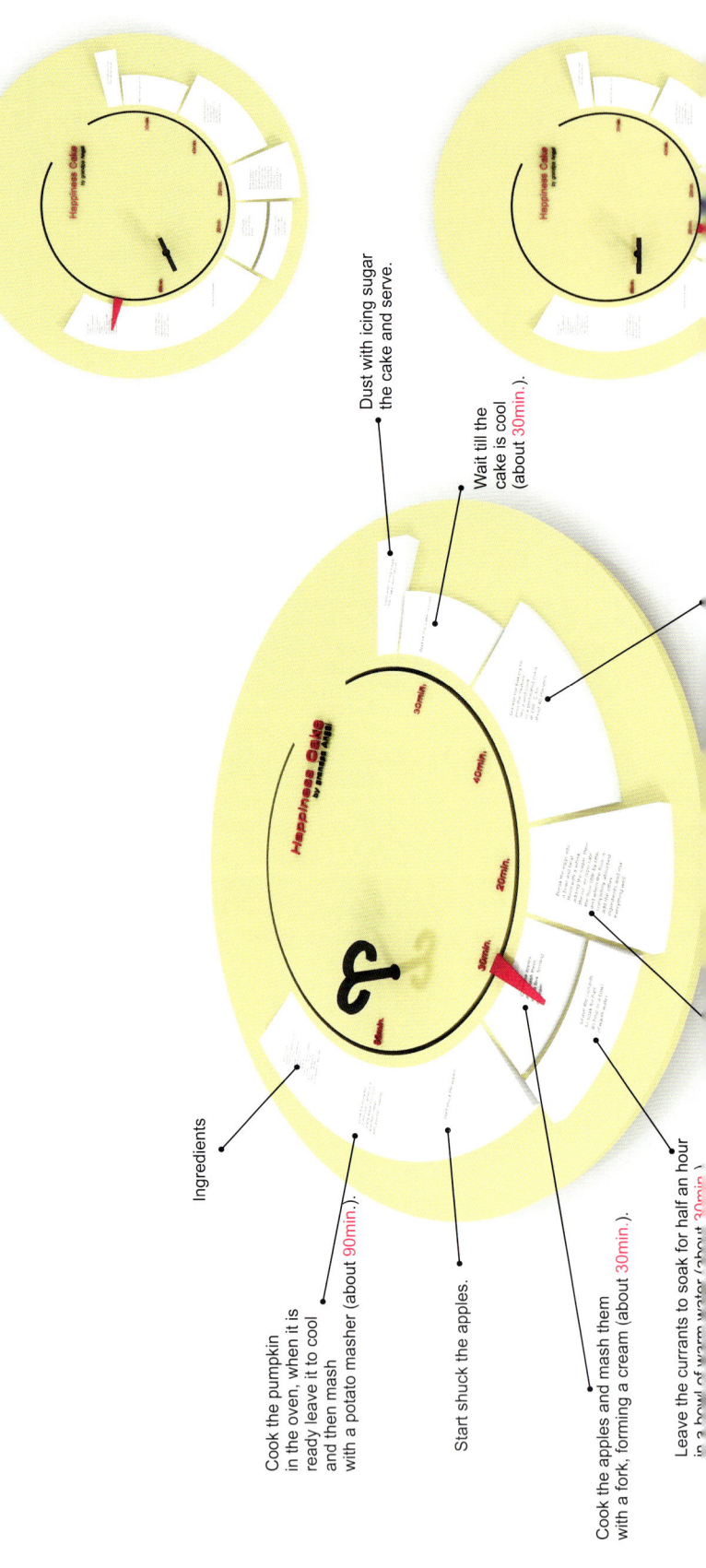

Dust with icing sugar the cake and serve.

Wait till the cake is cool (about 30min.).

Ingredients

Cook the pumpkin in the oven, when it is ready leave it to cool and then mash with a potato masher (about 90min.).

Start shuck the apples.

Cook the apples and mash them with a fork, forming a cream (about 30min.).

Leave the currants to soak for half an hour in a bowl of warm water (about 30min.).

Clockwork Cake Recipe

clink!!!

Heritage
The Clockwork Cake Recipe is a visual timing system that has been designed in order to simplify the recipe invented by Grandpa Angel to new generation of users. It's a physical recipe that can be transmitted over generation, not just a simple piece of paper. It becomes also a powerful visual image in a kitchen.

How it function:
The principle is very simple: All the primary baking operations are split up in visual fragments (include the ingredients) representing the timing. Start by turning the key and the clockwork start to work.
When a time operation is over a mechanical sound signal will announce you that.

Sustainable
The system is powered by a clockwork mechanism, using a key.
So is not using any type of battery, being environment friendly. Also this system can be repaired when is broken.

Timing
We live in an era of timing…usually we calculate every operation that we intend to make in a day, so we have the same problem with recipes.
The Clockwork Cake Recipe is more a coordinator of main operations, not an exact timing machine.
Even the video presentation of Grandma Beppa is not very explicit about timing of all the food operations.

Tourism
Becoming an object, the Clockwork Cake Recipe could be an important souvenir for tourists that visit the specific area of Grandma Beppa. Not to forget that recipe was invented by Grandpa Angel, the grandpa of Beppa, so it is already part of family heritage, and by extension of that Italian region - Veneto. Usually, if the tourists discover specific food of a region, they are asking for the recipe. Now they can take with them physically this recipe!

Material
Tin body, with clockwork mechanism.

on the wall

on the table

FOOD INSPIRES DESIGN

GRANDMA'S
LEMON TART
INSPIRES
THE DESIGNER
TO CREATE
SORRENTINA
LEMON
FUROSHIKI

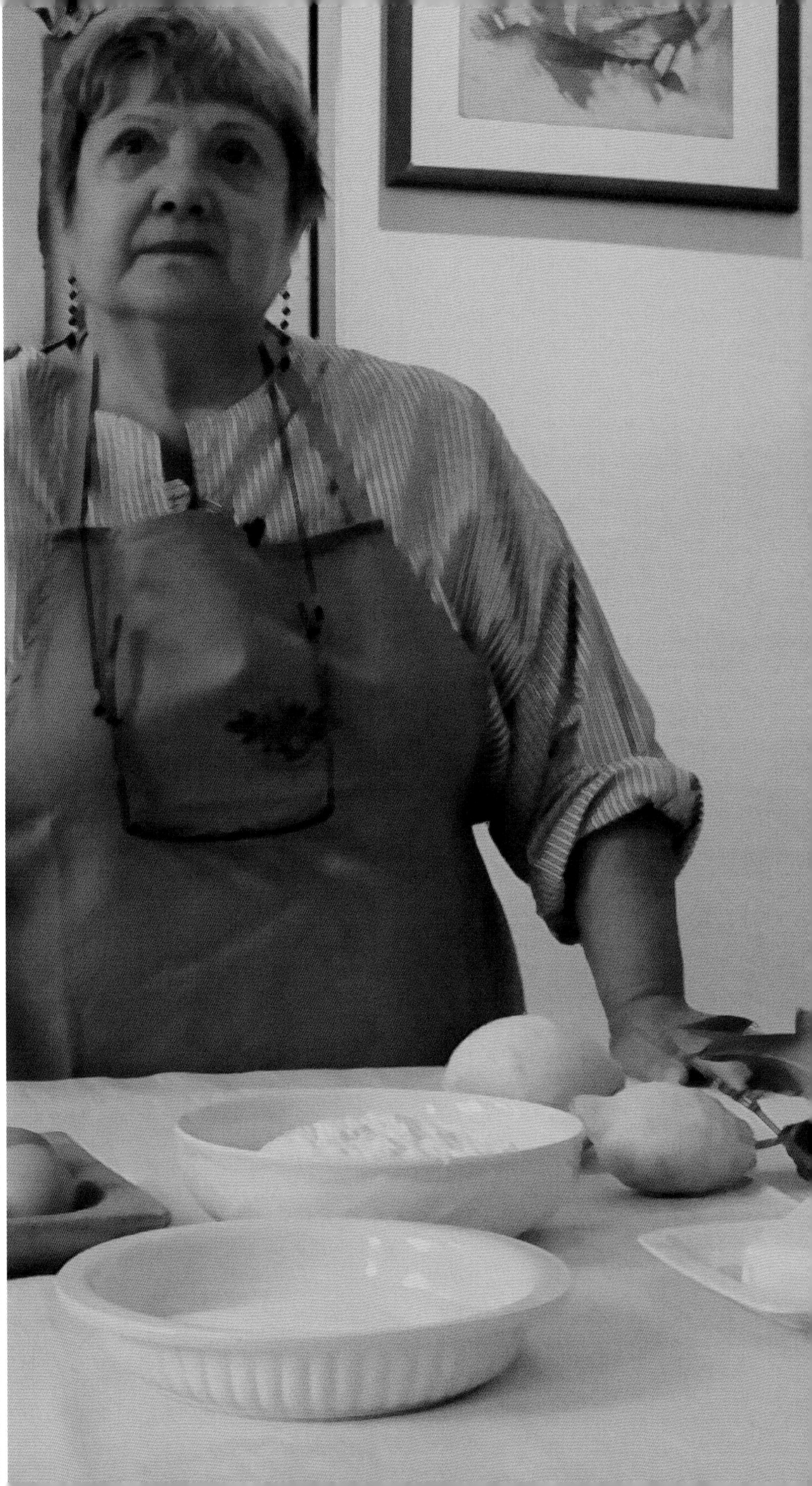

The Grandma

NAME
Lia

NAME
Lia

COUNTRY
Italy

RECIPE
Sorrentina Lemon Tart

LIA

Lia has worked in the United Nations, at the Food and Agriculture Organization, which was an opportunity to taste many types of cuisine and products: she particularly likes mango and sticky rice from Thailand, as well as papaya and lychees. As for Italian products, she loves lemons and especially the ones from the Sorrento coast as they have a unique taste.

RECIPE > HISTORY AND TRADITION
Lemons are a very common fruit in the Sorrento peninsula. They have been used since the 1800s, when lemonade made from this marvellous fruit was sold from little carts found on street corners.

SORRENTINA LEMON TART

INGREDIENTS

a baking tin

For the short crust pastry:
300g flour
150g butter
150g sugar
3 eggs
salt

For the lemon cream:
4 eggs yolks
130g sugar
200ml fresh pouring cream
2 lemons from Sorrento
lemon rind as required

PREPARATION

The short crust pastry. Use only chilled ingredients. Sieve the flour and the sugar onto a flat surface and make a hollow. Pour the egg yolks into the hollow and work into a homogeneous stiff dough. Once the dough is ready, form a ball, wrap it in cling film and chill in the refrigerator for about 30 minutes. Take the dough out of the fridge and roll out on a floured surface into a 1cm thick even disc shape. Place the dough into a greased and floured baking dish, removing the dough hanging over the edge of the dish. Heat the oven to 170°C.

The lemon cream:
In a mixing bowl whisk the egg yolks, sugar, pouring cream and the juice of the lemons for a few minutes. Pour the cream into the baking tin and garnish with small strips of half the lemon rind.
Bake in a preheated oven for 35 minutes. Just before the end of the cooking time, take out the tart, sprinkle with the remaining lemon rind and continue to cook for another 5 minutes.

The Designer

Dear Lia,
your Sorrentina Lemon tart
recipe inspired me to create a
Furoshiki cloth to wrap around
lemons or limoncello as a gift.
Designing the cloth allowed me to
evoke the sun and memories of
summer holidays past, and in
particular the summer I spent
working on a farm in Italy.

Thank you!

Alice x

NAME
Alice Dansey-Wright

COUNTRY
United Kingdom

EDUCATION
Glasgow School of Art
with a BA(hons) in Environmental Art

FIELD OF EXPERTISE
I've developed a more design-focused practice, working collaboratively with food and fashion creatives. My work encompasses illustration, graphic design, products, packaging, workshops and wall drawings. I'm inspired by folk art and lo-fi processes and I work largely in pen and ink and then develop my designs digitally

WEBSITE
http://cargocollective.com/alicedanseywright

The Concept

SORRENTINA LEMON FUROSHIKI

CATEGORY

Design About Food (DAF)

DESCRIPTION

My concept is a design for a Furoshiki cloth that celebrates Sorrento lemons, particularly their historical link with the Amalfi and Sorrento coasts and their use in the production of Limoncello. I came up with the Furoshiki cloth because I wanted to design something similar to a scarf in shape and layout but that could also be used for food. Furoshiki are traditional Japanese wrapping cloths used for food, clothes and gifts. It can be used as a scarf but also as a bag to take to the food market or for wrapping lemons, lemon tart/cake or Limoncello.

As an illustrator and surface pattern designer based in Glasgow, Scotland, much of my work revolves around textiles (especially silk scarves). I created the design from my home studio in Glasgow, generally a very cold and wet place with little sun. Designing the cloth allowed me to evoke the sun and memories of past summer holidays, particularly the summer I spent working on a farm in Italy. I'm currently very inspired by the 1980s textile design, which I think you can see in this work. This also goes hand-in-hand with my childhood memories of summer as I grew up in the 1980s, and in my memory the sun was always shining. I created the design by drawing onto a large square of white cartridge paper with black ink, then scanning this pattern into my computer and finally adding the colours digitally.

My concept is a design for a Furoshiki cloth that celebrates Lemons from Sorrento- their history and association with the Amalfi and Sorrento coasts and their use in the making of Limoncello

Sorrentina Lemon Furoshiki

Alice Dansey-Wright

Category: Design About Food
Grandma: Lia, Sorrentina Lemon Tart

I created the design from my home studio in Glasgow, Scotland- which is a generally very wet and cold place with little sun. Designing the cloth allowed me to evoke the sun and memories of Summer holidays past, and in particular the summer I spent working on a farm in Italy.

FOOD INSPIRES DESIGN

GRANDMA'S
PASTIERA
INSPIRES
THE DESIGNER
TO CREATE
PASTIERA

The Grandma

NAME
Franca

COUNTRY
Italy

RECIPE
Pastiera

RECIPE > HISTORY AND TRADITION

This dessert dates back to ancient times when the agricultural community prepared the cake in spring, possibly as a votive offering to the siren Partenope for her beautiful singing. Nowadays the cake is made at Easter. Franca's recipe was handed down to her by her mother. Variants include the use of different kinds of grain, and even pasta. Orange flower essence may also be added. Be careful however, for a bottle can cost up to 2,000 Euros.

The Recipe

PASTIERA

INGREDIENTS

a baking tin

For the short crust pastry:
125g chilled butter
250g flour
a pinch of salt
100g sugar
1 egg and 1 egg yolk

For the filling:
350g ricotta
4 eggs, separated
1 spoon cinnamon
rind of 1 lemon
1 packet of vanilla essence
250g wheat grain boiled in milk
80g candied fruit
350g sugar
icing sugar

PREPARATION

First prepare the short crust pastry:
Cut the butter (just taken out of the refrigerator and well chilled) into small pieces and rub into the flour with a pinch of salt so that it resembles breadcrumbs.
Then add the sugar. Form a hollow, add the egg yolks, and combine the flour with the yolks.
Add the egg white and knead lightly to form an elastic dough.
Wrap in cling film and leave to rest in the refrigerator for at least 40 minutes.

The filling:
Blend the ricotta. Add the 4 egg yolks. Stir in the cinnamon, the grated lemon rind and the powdered vanilla essence.
Mix in the boiled wheat grain. Add the candied fruit.
Whisk the egg whites and sugar into stiff peaks and then fold them in gently.

Press the short crust pastry into the baking tin.
Add the filling. Bake the tart at 180°C for about an hour or until the top is golden brown.
Finish by dusting with icing sugar.

The Designer

NAME & COUNTRY
Antonella Mignacca, Italy

EDUCATION
Course at the Polytechnic of Milan
in Food Experience Design

FIELD OF EXPERTISE
Food design

WEBSITE
www.intothefood.eu

The Concept

PASTIERA

CATEGORY

Design With Food (DWF)

DESCRIPTION

I am very devoted to the pastiera because I was born in the same region. My version is a tribute to Naples with its volcano Mount Vesuvius. I wanted to change not only the shape but also the consistency and flavour of the pastiera.
During the preparation, the volcano seems to come to life and then, just like in the legend, Partenope transforms the ingredients with her magic singing. I believe that food not only serves as survival. There are many culinary traditions all over the world and over the course of time, almost every region and section of the population has developed its own specialities. Eating is an experience to which we ascribe emotions and meanings, all of which often extend further than the food itself. Food draws us together and food distinguishes us. I still continue to study, work and experiment with food. My motto is: "Design with your stomach, eat with love!"

ORANGE FLOWER ESSECE

MILK

SUGAR

EGG YOLKS

ORANGE FLOWER ESSECE

SALT

LEMON
GRATED

FLOUR
SIEVED

2 - WORK IT TOGE
MAKE IT INT

CLINGFILM

3 - PREPARE AND BAKE THE

GREASE THE FUNNEL OF STEEL

ROLL OUT
THE PASTRY

THIS DESSERT DATES BACK TO ANCIENT TIMES WHEN THE AGRICULTURAL COMMUNITY PREPARED THIS CAKE IN SPRING POSSIBLY AS A VOTIVE OFFERING TO THE SIREN PARTENOPE.

THERE'S A LEGEND THAT THE TRADITION STARTED BECAUSE THE INHABITANTS WANTED TO GIVE THANKS TO PARTENOPE FOR HER BEAUTIFUL SINGING.

NOWADAYS THIS CAKE IS PREPARED AT EASTER.

Pastiera
NAPLES, Italy

INGREDIENTS

FOR THE SHORTCRUST PASTRY
BUTTER 125G
FLOUR 250G
1 EGG AND ONE YOLK
SUGAR 100G

FOR THE FILLING
GRAIN BOILED IN MILK 250G
RICOTTA 350G
SUGAR ICING 250 G
1 SPOON CINNAMON
CANDIED FRUIT 80 G

FOR THE PASTRY CREAM
EGG YOLKS 5
PEEL OF 1 LEMON
MILK
ORANGE FLOWER ESSENCE
SUGAR 125G

THE SHORTCRUST PASTRY

SUGAR

EGG YOLKS
EGG WHITE

BUTTER
CUT INTO CUBES

1 - PREPARE THE FILL OF THE VUOLCANOES

ORANGE FLOWER ESSECE

EGG YOLKS

ORANGE FLOWER ESSECE

MILK

SUGAR

CINNAMON

GRAIN

MILK

ICING SUGAR

CANDIED FRUIT

RICOTTA

BOIL AND AFTER TO MILL IT.

REPOSE

VUOLCANOES
30 MIN - 150°

CUT INTO A STRIP THE PASTRY AND WRAP THE FUNNEL

5 - MAKE THE PASTRY CREAM AND POUR ON THE VUOLCANOES

GOOD TASTE!

FOOD INSPIRES DESIGN

GRANDMA'S
CALABRESE PIZZA
INSPIRES
THE DESIGNER
TO CREATE
FRAY

The Grandma

RECIPE > HISTORY AND TRADITION

Silvana is originally from Calabria, concretely from Catanzaro. Both the recipe, which is called Calabrese pizza, or pitta 'mpigliata' and her mother-in-law originate from the province of Cosenza. The dessert is traditionally prepared at Christmas and her mother-in-law was particularly good at making it. She used a type of wine called vincotto, produced from the must of the grapes and concentrated by cooking at a high temperature for a long period. It was specifically kept aside for use in the Christmas pizza. So many Calabrese pizzas were made at Christmas that they lasted for the whole year; each family made six or seven.

CALABRESE PIZZA

INGREDIENTS

a baking tin

For the dough:
1kg flour
2 eggs
200g sugar
a glass of olive oil
a glass of Vermouth

For the filling:
200g almonds
200g walnuts
candied orange pieces
raisins
sugar
cloves
chopped cinnamon
a glass of aromatic liquor ("Strega")
honey

PREPARATION

The filling:
Mix the walnuts broken up into small pieces, the chopped almonds, the candied orange, the spices and the sugar in a bowl. Then add the liquor.
Leave to rest for at least a quarter of an hour.

The dough:
Pour the flour onto a flat surface; add the sugar, eggs, oil and Vermouth. Knead the ingredients. Cut the dough in half.
Roll out one half to make a layer for the bottom of the tart.
Roll out the other half to make strips of dough.

Place the bottom layer into a greased baking tin, add the filling and arrange the strips of dough on top.
These can be rolled to produce a rose effect.
Bake in the oven at 150°C for 50 minutes.
Once cooked, drizzle with honey that has been melted in a bain-marie.

The Designer

NAME & COUNTRY

Juliana Mendonça,
Renata Dias and Larissa Grace
(Voglio Design), Brazil

EDUCATION

State University of Minas Gerais

Juliana: Degree in Law and Product Design
and expertise in business management
Renata: Product Design
Larissa: Interior Design

FIELD OF EXPERTISE

Developing projects associated with food
consumption, utensils and food itself.

WEBSITE

www.vogliodesign.com

Dear Silvana,

Thanks a lot for teaching us culinary culture. It was really you cooking, listen to your stories more of you.

It was really important for of our concept to see you cooking, was based on your gestures while preparing the food and how you manipulate the dough. Aiming to add even more value to the cultural aspects of the recipe, the product was developed to make the act of cooking easier and with a nice presentation, with practical tools that can also be used as beautiful frames.

Thanks again for inspiring us and give us the chance of being part of this great competition.

Kind regards,

Juliana, Renata, Larissa

The Concept

FRAY

CATEGORY

Design For Food (DFF)

DESCRIPTION

Our aim is to develop a utensil that will make the recipe presentation more attractive, as well as making it easier to serve.
The product is comprised of frames that can be used with the baking tray already on sale on the market (the ones with removable bases). Besides showing off the food served, when it's not being used for this function, it can be hung on the wall, forming part of the room's decoration. To facilitate serving the food, the frames have crimps that guide the knife when slicing the pizza.

CALABRESE PIZZA
GRANDMA: SILVANA
COUNTRY: ITALY
ORIGIN: CALABRIA

FRAY

VIDEO OBSERVATIONS:

- Traditional Christmas dessert;

- The presentation of the product is all handmade;

- Silvana, after finishing the recipe, exchange the tray for a more beautiful one.

Importance of valuing the presentation of the recipe

Valorizing the APPEARANCE

Art + Italian Culture

Famous painters

Remarkable paintings

Use of frames to PROTECT and VALORIZE even more the piece in the environment

Concept: "ART IN THE KITCHEN"

Proposal: development of a utensil that will make the presentation of the recipe more attractive, besides facilitating the moment of serving - DESIGN FOR FOOD.

DESCRIPTION OF THE PRODUCT:
Frames that can be used with the baking tray already sell in the market (the ones that loose the botton).
Besides standing out the food served, when its not in use with this function, it can be fixed on the wall and be part of the decoration of the room.
To facilitate the moment os serving, the frames have crimps that orientate the knife for slicing the pizza.

FOOD INSPIRES DESIGN

GRANDMA'S
SPECULAAS
FROM HASSELT
INSPIRES
THE DESIGNER
TO CREATE
MAGDA

The Grandma

NAME
Magda

COUNTRY
Belgium

RECIPE
Speculaas from Hasselt

MAGDA

According to Magda, speculaas are far too expensive at the bakery, so she started to make them herself. She got some advice from Fernande Deplée, the daughter of a very famous baker in Hasselt, called Josephe Antoine Deplee. He grew up in a family of liqueur distillers and was the first to add liqueur to the recipe, in 1870. He even acquired a licence for Hasseltse speculaas: "une espèce de pain d'amandes connu sous le nom de spéculation" (a kind of almond bread known by the name of speculation). He sold his speculaas in Belgium and also abroad, becoming one of the most famous bakers of Hasselt before the World War I . Fernande Deplée and Magda were very good friends. Following Fernande's advice, Magda started experimenting. After a couple of years and much trial-and-error, she finally found the perfect recipe.

RECIPE > HISTORY AND TRADITION

Many bakeries in Hasselt claim to have the oldest recipe, although its origins are questionable. Research has recently shown that Hasselt already had speculaas in the 1830s. The Hasselt bakeries offered a crusty brown cake to the Belgian Army soldiers, when they were on their way to the independence war with the Netherlands. Another story is that the delicacy has its origins in the dozens of Jenever distilleries in Hasselt, which had a lot of sugar leftovers. Brown sugar is made from partially burned sugar. If you mix this sugar with flour and butter, you will understand how speculaas were born. Not only is the origin of the speculaas questionable, the history of the name is uncertain as well. One interpretation involves "species", a bastardization of "épices" (French for spices). Speculaas became famous in Belgium and abroad during the late 19th and early 20th Centuries, mainly due to the achievement of Josephe Antoine Deplée. Most of the recipes stayed in families and were passed down from fathers to sons. One thing is for sure: The way you handle the dough is very important. As Magda indicates herself: "It's all in the kneading."

The Recipe

HASSELTSE SPECULAAS

INGREDIENTS

1kg flour
700g dark brown sugar
1 tsp cinnamon
1 tsp bicarbonate of soda
300g butter
4 eggs
almonds
Wissels Jenever, a kind of Belgian gin

PREPARATION

The day before:
Mix the flour with the sugar. Add the cinnamon and
bicarbonate of soda. Divide the butter into cubes and
incorporate in the dough. Add the egg yolks.
Knead until the dough is elastic and smooth.
Whisk the egg white and gently fold into the mixture.
Finally, add the almonds and gin. Mix well, cover,
and leave to rest for one night.

The next morning:
Heat the oven to 195°C.
Knead the dough again. Divide into small pieces and
make little biscuits.
Place the biscuits on a baking tray and place it
in the preheated oven for 17 minutes.
Take the speculaas out of the oven, allow to cool
and serve with a good cup of coffee.

The Designer

NAME & COUNTRY
Julie Ganaye and Marine Hérisson, France

EDUCATION
In last year of a five-year Master's Degree in
Graphic and Product Design in the New Eating
Habits option at L'École de design Nantes
Atlantique in France

FIELD OF EXPERTISE
Product design and graphic design

CONTACT
marineherisson@neuf.fr

n recipe " Speculaas from Hasselt " inspires us for our
jict. What's more it seemed to be the tastiest one and
n personal story about this recipe had sensibilize us.

will explain our product on few words :
name of the product is Jagda, it's a bottle, the shape i
ined of your traditional bottle of Hasselt.
s bottle have 3 parts, each for one main ingredients :
sselt alcohol, cinnamon wood and ceramic to keep th
ditional and handmade aspect.
at's more on a attached paper, we have all the exp
story. We also create a logo " Jada

The Concept

MAGDA

CATEGORY

DFF

DESCRIPTION

We chose Magda's recipe of 'speculaas' because it seemed to be the tastiest one. Adding to that, it was easier to create something related to what she wanted to communicate because she explains the recipe's background very well: one of the most difficult aspects of the recipe was finding the perfect measures. That is why we created a bottle with different compartments to put the specific ingredients (like alcohol and cinnamon) in the right measure, enabling anyone to make the recipe as Magda does.

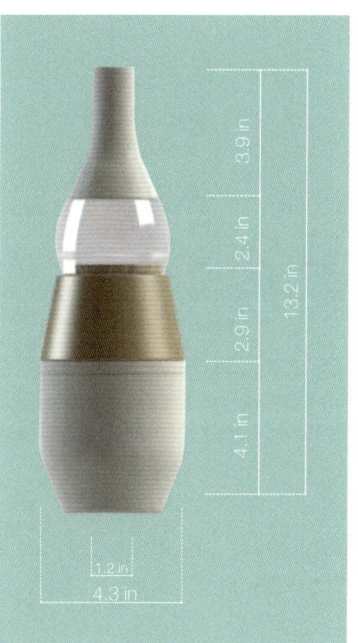

MAGDA

By Marine Hérisson & Julie Ganaye

We are product design and graphic design students in France and we decided to create a product for this competition. So we choose «Speculaas» from Hasselt», Magda's recipe, which come from Belgium. Magda's video seemed to be the tastiest one. She speak a lot about the story of the recipe so it's was more easy to create something in relation with what she want to communicate. In her recipe she use a lot of HASSELT TYPICAL ingredient like alcohol or cinnamon. So we create an bottle with which you can remake the same recipe as Magda.

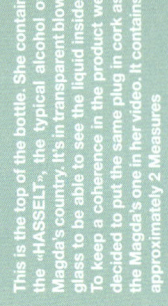
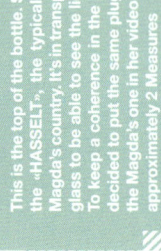

1 This is the top of the bottle. She contain the «HASSELT», the typical alcohol of Magda's country. It's in transparent blow glass to be able to see the liquid inside. To keep a coherence in the product we decided to put the same plug in cork as the Magda's one in her video. It contains approximately 2 Measures

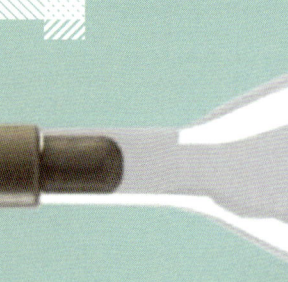

2 In her video Magda uses a very famous alcohol in Belgium : «HASSELT». She put in her recipe 1 glass of this alcohol. So This plug is create to put 1 measure in the recipe. The material is ceramics (white). We have choose to hang on a label which containing all the ingredients in the recipe and the recipe. We also create a logo «Magda» to give a real identity and afterthat be able to marketed

3

In this part of the bottle you find the cinnamon and the almonds. The used material is the birch wood. two main ingredients in the recipe that you cannot find everywhere. You have more than 2 measure but the goal of the bottle is to be re-use endlessly.

4

And finally in this part you find the brown sugar. The main ingredient in the speculaas. Even if it's an ingredient which we can find everywhere,we find it very interesting to put in the bottle. Like number 2 the used material is creamic to recall the ancestral aspect of the recipe.

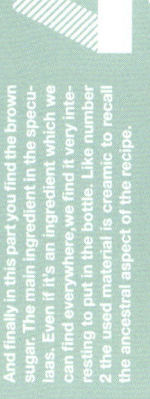

MAGDA

A BELGIAN RECIPE

The Jury

The Grandma' Design jury was comprised of notable food designers, consultants and lecturers from Europe: Anna Cerrocchi (Italy), Francesca Zampollo (Italy), Karlijn Souren (the Netherlands), Marc Bretillot (France), Morgaine Gaye (UK)

ANNA CERROCCHI

Anna's professional studio, ONE Off, was the first in Europe to conceive a public event focused on food design (2002: first competition launch). In ten years they organized six editions of the event Food design®. More than 1000 people came from all over the world answered to the calls for applications; 250 new projects were selected and exhibited on several occasions all over the world.

During these years they have extended the network of creative people working on food design, working together to identify their particular research, focused on the project of food and on everything that revolves around food: Utensils, packaging, models and rituals of consumption... The expertise acquired also facilitated contacts and collaborations with several companies in the world of food.

Since 2006 she has been a member of the Permanent Design Observatory (ADI – Associazione per il Disegno Industriale), selecting the best food design projects for the ADI Index (annual report on the best Italian products). In recent years she has led or taken part in several workshops and conferences on food design. As a lecturer at the Polytechnic of Turin she has also supervised several students in their design graduation works based on food design projects.
www.food-design.it

FRANCESCA ZAMPOLLO

Francesca is a design researcher and a food design consultant with a background in industrial design. She is an award winning food designer, with her most successful product, the chocolate snack Unico, in production since 2006. Francesca founded the International Food Design Society in 2009, and has since organised the First International Symposium on Food Experience Design (November 2010) and the International Conference on Designing Food and Designing for Food (June 2012), the first academic conference on Food Design. She is a part-time lecturer at the London Metropolitan University where she runs the studio Meaningful Food, designed for product and furniture design students.
http://francesca-zampollo.com

KARLIJN SOUREN

Karlijn Souren is a designer with a fascination for daily rituals in general and the ritual of eating in particular. She graduated as a product designer from the Utrecht School of the Arts (HKU) in 2006.

After completing her studies she worked for two years as a junior designer at Marije Vogelzang's Proef, where she was able to further develop her expertise in eating design.
From 2007 to 2009 she teamed up with Anna Brecht and they developed eating concepts and food designs for various events and organisations under the name of Everything But a Slice of Bread.
Karlijn has run workshops and given lectures for various faculties of the Utrecht School of the Arts, the University of Applied Sciences Utrecht (HU), the Association of Dutch Designers (BNO), ArtEZ and different secondary schools.
In September 2012, the book "Watertanden" (Mouth Watering) was published, which she created in collaboration with Renske de Greef and Andreia Costa. The book culminates creative research on the way food shapes our lives. In five chapters she introduces the role of food in the five stages of our lives and proposes new and innovative designs that deepen or extend this role.
Currently, her focus is on developing food concepts for non-profit organisations. She has worked and works for Pallas Athene College Ede, Princes Máxima Centre for Children's Oncology and Vrede van Utrecht among others. Next to this she joined Creative Chef, an interdisciplinary team of young professionals creating new concepts for exploring the experience of eating.
www.karlijnsouren.nl

MARC BRETILLOT

Marc Bretillot is a food designer. As well as catering and artisan culinary practices, the creation of new products, innovation consulting for the food industry, he also organises international events and performances for galleries and museums. He is the director of the Masters Programme and created the Post-graduate Degree of Culinary Design at the Art & Design University of Reims (ESAD), which is where his adventure began when he created the first research workshop on culinary design in 1999. He gives conferences at the prestigious cookery school, l'École Française de Gastronomie in Paris and is also invited to give workshops in France and abroad. He is the co-author of "Culinaire Design" published by Alternatives and is currently developing an online platform called www.thinkingfooddesign.com which brings together industrialists, chefs, designers, historians and anyone else who is passionate about... food.
www.marcbretillot.com

MORGAINE GAYE

As a food futurologist, Morgaine Gaye looks at food and eating from a social, cultural, economic, trend, branding and geo-political perspective. Her work involves consulting to food companies that use her research to develop new products or campaigns. She writes articles and trend reports for PR/advertising agencies and publications. She gives academic lectures within a university context and also corporate lectures on specific food trends. Developing new ideas for food-related TV programmes which she normally presents is another element of her job. She researches all the elements of the eating experience from taste to mouth-feel and olfactory perceptions.
www.morgainegaye.com

Thanks to the support of

This project has been funded with support from the European Commission.
This publication reflects the views only of the author, and the Commission cannot be
held responsible for any use which may be made of the information contained therein.

The partners

Hogeschool van Amsterdam (The Netherlands)
Yeditepe University (Turkey)
National Consumer Research Centre (Finland)
International Food Design Society

Published on the occasion of
Grandma's Design, see www.grandmasdesign.com

Texts by
Francesca Zampollo and others

Coordination
Steven Cleeren
Annelore Smits

Book Concept
Design Vlaanderen
Npo Vol-au-vent

Photo Credits
Pieter De Clercq (Belgium)
Özge Samanci (Turkey)
Beppe Leonetti (DERIVA FILM), Alberto Carraro (AICM)
and others

Final Editing
Sally-Ann Hopwood

Layout
Inge Van Damme, www.ingedingen.be

Printed by
www.pureprint.be

Published by
Stichting Kunstboek
Legeweg 165
B-8020 Oostkamp
www.stichtingkunstboek.com

ISBN: 978-90-5856-475-7
NUR: 656/442
D/2013/6407/39